CW00520716

PEARL HARBOR
STILL SHOCKING
80 YEARS ON

51 startling facts about history's biggest surprise attack

BENEDICT LE VAY

A **One Particular House** Minibook

One Particular House, London. 'Easier to find than Random House'

Copyright © 2021 Benedict le Vay

All rights reserved.

ISBN: 9798654422989

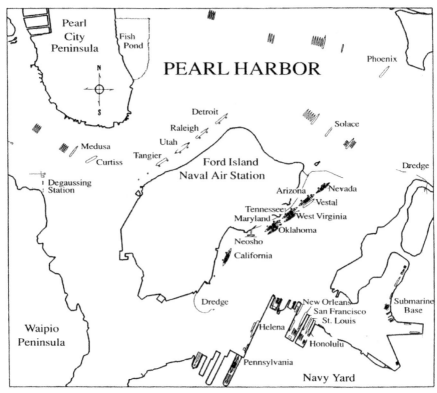

Positions of the major ships. Chart courtesy: National Park Service

DEDICATION

For every single American, and indeed Allied, soldier, sailor or airman who fought in the horrendous war against Japan, 1941-45. And in everlasting gratitude that the United States, and the Soviet Union, joined the global struggle against evil. The war couldn't have been won otherwise.

ACKNOWLEDGMENTS

James F. Lansdale, Robin Popham, Wendy Fuller, U.S. Navy, Wikimedia, Japan Times, Ceylon Daily News. Tech Sgt Ben Bloker (picture of Lightning), National Park Service, Asahi Shimbun, U.S. Military Academy, Kelvin Wynne, Richard Levay, Lawrence Webb, Jeff Shaw, Canadian Aviation and Space Museum, Australian War Memorial, Maine Department of Agriculture, Conservation and Forestry, The Economist, Illustrated London News, William S. Smith, Encyclopedia of Arkansas History and Culture. Any mistakes are, however, my own. Please do contact me with comments at benlevay@aol.com

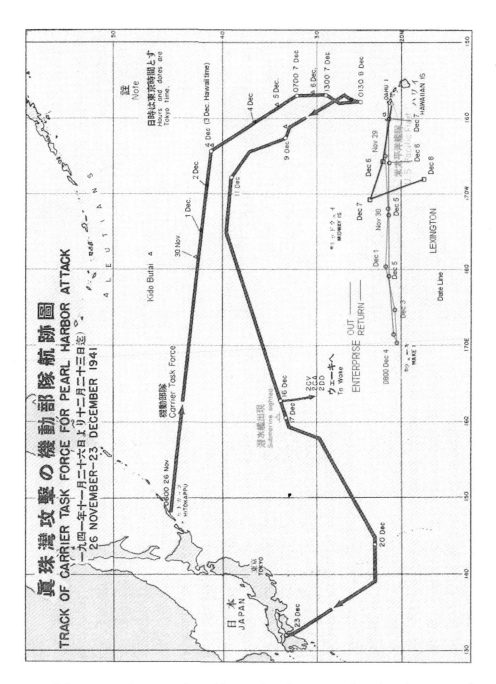

A Japanese chart, produced long after the event, showing the route of
the aircraft carrier task force to Hawaii (thick black line). The lighter
lines are the positions of U.S. carriers

The USS West Virginia and the USS Tennessee burn in the attack

CONTENTS

Dedication & Acknowledgments   ii

PART ONE

History's most famous surprise attack   5

Fifty-one surprises about that attack   6

PART TWO

Bonus Chapters: Unlikely Wars, etc   84

About the author   107

By the same author   108

HISTORY'S MOST FAMOUS SURPRISE ATTACK: PEARL HARBOR

WE already know all about Pearl Harbor, don't we? You will have gleaned from countless books, TV programmes, movies and school history lessons these essentials:

That the 'day of infamy' (as President Roosevelt put it) was the shocking first blow by the Japanese in World War II; an attack without any warning; that this caused America to declare war on Hitler and his allies; that the sad fate of the ships moored at Pearl Harbor that day was entirely the fault of the Japanese; that the Japanese taught themselves how to use aircraft carriers offensively with their effective armour-piercing bombs; that they were led by a brilliant admiral who wanted to strike the first blow against the USA; that there was no Japanese landing or invasion of Hawaii and no repeat of the unique attack on Pearl Harbor; that several battleships being lost or damaged greatly hampered the U.S. in the ensuing war; that only the American aircraft carriers and submarines which miraculously escaped the attack brought about the eventual defeat of the Imperial Japanese Navy, starting with brilliant torpedo plane attacks on carriers, and quick, effective attacks by U.S. submarines.

Except for one thing. *Every 'fact' in the preceding paragraph is wrong.* And finding out why is utterly fascinating.

It should first be said that it WAS an appalling, sneak attack that changed history. It has been compared to the 9/11 attacks in 2001, when again the sleeping dragon of the USA was hit hard and woke with a mighty roar, lashing out. Pearl Harbor certainly catapulted America into the war, ensuring the eventual defeat of Nazi Germany and precipitated the destruction of the glittering British Empire in the Far East. A sun rising on one empire ... and setting on another.

Its effects were further reaching as it propelled the hitherto isolationist USA into taking over Britain's 'global policeman' role, with the world's biggest military intervening around the globe, for good or ill, until the present day. Without Pearl Harbor, would the Korean and Vietnam wars have happened, or lasted as long?

It also – and this will be a less popular statement in some quarters – disabused us of the idea that Asian people are necessarily backward and unable to stand up to the technologically superior

Western colonial powers. That white people are superior, to put it bluntly, and what were mocked as bamboo planes flown by somehow more primitive people will never prevail against mighty Western forces. How wrong that turned out to be. (Nor would I be so naïve as to think Asian people were not capable of being racist and consider themselves superior – that was part of the problem too).

But you knew all that, didn't you? What you may *not* have known is these strangely fascinating details which will make you think again about that shattering day:

1 It *wasn't* the very start of Japan's war

ALL the history books say the attack on Pearl Harbor on Sunday, December 7, 1941 marked the very first Japanese entry into the war. It wasn't. Actually the Japanese attacks on British positions in Malaya (now Malaysia) on Monday, December 8 came 15 minutes *earlier* because of the effect of the international date line between the two. This is clearer when you look at Japanese timings – they considered the Pearl Harbor attack as also on December 8 (by Tokio time).

In a picture taken from an attacking aircraft, a torpedo is seen striking the USS West Virginia in 'Battleship Row' on the far side of Ford Island. To the right of the waterspout can just be made out a Japanese plane in action

2 There *was* plenty of warning…

IF it was one of history's greatest surprise attacks, it certainly needn't have been. Ten days beforehand, an official warning had been sent to West Coast installations that an attack was likely. I quote from an order marked 'Secret' and issued on November 28: 'The future action of Japan cannot be predicted, but surprise aggressive action at any moment is possible.' An hour before the actual attack, a prowling Japanese midget submarine was sunk by naval gunfire at the harbour entrance, and others were seen trying to attack, and one ran aground.

Amazingly, the anti-submarine nets had been left open because a ship's arrival was expected much later! A few minutes later a trainee at an aircraft warning station at Opana Point told his commanding officer that a large force of aircraft was approaching from 130 miles to the north-east but this was discounted as unimportant (possibly because U.S. bombers flying in from the mainland were expected, and because the naïve radar operators thought the approach was from the wrong direction for a Japanese attack). No alarm was raised, the submarine net remained open and the coastal guns and ship anti-aircraft positions unmanned. As a direct consequence, in the next two hours America suffered 2,403 servicemen killed, nearly 200 aircraft destroyed and seven battleships sunk or crippled.

The Opana Point radar site spotted the coming raid, but nothing was done

3 ... the spying was unsubtle ...

THE vital pieces of equipment the key Japanese spy in Hawaii used to track the U.S. fleet were hardly cloak and dagger or high-tech... two eyeballs and a pencil. Takeo Yoshikawa regularly strolled to the end of Pearl City Peninsula jutting into the harbour noting down the names of ships in his book. If that wasn't obvious enough, if in doubt he would hire a light plane and swoop low over the ships taking pictures. OK, he wasn't towing a banner warning of the attack, but pretty close.

4 Even the local paper made it clear

I WAS going to write in the last item: 'What more did the Japanese have to do – advertise it in the local newspapers?' but then I looked at the front page of the *Honolulu Advertiser* of November 30, 1941, a week before the attack. Across the top of the page it says:

Japanese May Strike Over Weekend!

Which they certainly did.

The main banner headline was:

KURUSU BLUNTLY WARNED
NATION READY FOR BATTLE

Which it certainly wasn't on the day. Kurusu was the Japanese diplomat in Washington negotiating for peace, supposedly, even while the attack was starting. 'Ready for battle' seems a bit rich given the layers of warnings even on the day (item 2 above).

5 Who taught Japan how to do it?

A DISPLAY of British brilliance finally convinced the Japanese they could technically attack the American Pacific Fleet *inside* Pearl Harbor, much easier than finding ships all over the vast Pacific. In November 1940, Commander Minoru Genda, assistant Japanese air attaché in London, sent his masters a series of detailed reports with diagrams on the Fleet Air Arm's devastating attack on the Italian Fleet at Taranto.

The Japanese legation in Rome had sent representatives down to inspect the damage and any weaponry they could see. Orders went out to the Japanese forces to copy the tactics of low-level attacks with torpedoes adapted with fins, just as the British had, to run in shallow waters. Without these, torpedoes would have gone straight into the sea bed and this is the problem – harbours generally have far more shallows than deep channels.

6 ... and how to use aircraft carriers at all

ALTHOUGH the Americans were early to try launching aircraft off a ship – in 1910, only seven years after Wright brothers' first flimsy canvas and wood aircraft staggered into the air for a feeble flight shorter than the wingspan of today's jumbo jets – the first purpose-built aircraft carrier with a flush deck (a 'flat top') was laid down by the British, who had already used a converted ship for such a purpose during World War I.

They were then allies with the Japanese and exchanged technology, with Japanese naval experts visiting the RN's ships and shipyards. This British *HMS Hermes* was completed in 1924, and its Japanese imitator, the *Hosho*, was in fact first to be finished in 1922, albeit with some British and American equipment fitted. The closeness of the Royal Navy and its future enemy, the Imperial Japanese Navy has long been forgotten, but the Japanese admired Britain's 'Senior Service', the biggest Navy in the world. It is no coincidence that the IJN's flag echoes the RN's White Ensign and simple red and white design, and that its ranks, signal flags and methods were in some ways very similar.

And as for that infamous attack on Singapore at the time of Pearl Harbor in World War II, much is made of the Japanese knowing the lay-out of the harbor and defences through careful spying. Well, who had the British asked to help guard Singapore in World War I? Their allies, the Japanese.

The world's first purpose-built aircraft carrier, HMS Hermes, was launched in 1919 by the British, who shared expertise with their then Japanese allies

In 1915, Japanese troops helped the British put down a mutiny in Singapore. In that war, they escorted the ANZAC troop ships across the Indian Ocean, helped hunt down German raiders in co-operation with the Royal Navy, and even backed up Britain with a flotilla of 14 destroyers to base at Malta in 1917 and help escort convoys past German submarine threats.

That first Japanese carrier the *Hosho* was pretty obsolete by World War II and played a minor role in various battles, mostly being reserved for training. But unlike her more famous – or infamous – younger sisters who attacked Pearl Harbor and elsewhere, she survived the war and performed her most useful role after the atom bomb forced Japan to surrender, ferrying thousands of Japanese servicemen home from the various lands they had invaded.

7 ... and caused them to attack colonies?

A BRITISH bungle encouraged the Japanese to leap into the war when a top secret Cabinet paper saying the Far East colonies were all but defenceless was allowed to fall into enemy hands. Instead of being sent to Singapore in cipher by flying boat, it went in plain English in the steamer *Automeddon* which was attacked by a German raider off the Nicobar Islands in the Indian Ocean. Everyone on the bridge was killed by a shell, so the crew could not throw the weighted pouch overboard. The Germans' intelligence officer was hardly put off by it being marked sternly: 'British master only' and passed the material to the Japanese.

8 The reluctant first prisoner-of-war

FIVE *Ko-hyoteki* class Japanese midget submarines were launched from full-sized ones outside Pearl Harbor in the night before the air attack, each crewed by two men and with two torpedoes. One was sunk by naval gunfire from the *USS Ward* at 0637 that morning, the first shots of the Pacific war. One or two may have got into the harbour and fired their weapons during the attack, but nine of the ten men died. One crew member of a minisub that ran aground (pictured), Kazuo Samaki, aged 23, was captured but only because he became unconscious in the wreck – he would have preferred suicide, he made clear in hospital later. He thus became the Pacific war's first PoW and survived the war to become a pacifist businessman. The midget subs attacked Sydney, Australia, on May 29, 1942, and a harbour in Madagascar on the same date, with mixed results.

9 Holy ****!

MYTH says a ship's chaplain was setting up for morning service when it all started. He grabbed a heavy machine-gun and using the lectern as a prop, let rip, yelling 'Praise the Lord and pass the ammunition!' It was made into a popular song. That priest later denied it. However a chaplain on the New Orleans *did* say it to encourage men who carrying heavy shells, without fighting himself.

10 The joyful attacker

'MY HEART was ablaze with joy,' recalled the man who led the 360 attack aircraft. Air Staff Officer Mitsuo Fuchida (pictured) said: 'This was the high point of my career.' He turned up in America less than 20 years later – to preach forgiveness, as a Christian convert. Well, he would have been unwise to preach *not* forgiving.

11 The way men met macabre fates

The course of one macabre, dramatic attack can be told from startling start to horrifying finish because of multiple witnesses' accounts, (I am much indebted here to James F. Lansdale).

Let us look at the story of just one Japanese airman, Petty Officer Takashi Hirano, first class, who at about 0530 climbed into the cockpit of his Zero, No AI-154 aboard the carrier *Akagi*, 220 miles north of the Hawaiian island of Oahau. He and the other pilots had earlier gathered round to be briefed by a commander.

At 0550 as the six carriers swung east into the wind and the ships'

engines built up to maximum revs – to decrease take-off speed needed for the loaded aircraft – the aircraft engines were started and of his flight of nine Zeros, Hirano's *shotai* (element of three) was the first to take off. They reached the north-west coast of Oahu within two hours, as planned, escorting bombers from the carrier *Shakaku*. They flew south along the western slopes of the Ko'olau Mountain range.

Sitting ducks: The unarmed B-17s arrived to find themselves in the midst of a shooting war, with hundreds of Japanese planes looking for targets

Meanwhile, tired U.S. bomber crews were bringing in unarmed bombers after a 15-hour peaceful flight from California, en route to the Philippines, with no idea about what they were about to get mixed up in. It all seemed as peaceful as the name Pacific suggests. Their nation wasn't at war – for the next few minutes.

One of the 12 Boeing B-17s was rounding Diamond Head on the south shore. The co-pilot was member 2nd Lt. Ernest L. Reid. The unit's doctor was a passenger. Reid later described what he saw that utterly extraordinary day:

We caught our first glimpse of land. It was Diamond Head, a welcome sight. We all looked forward to spending the rest of the day on the beach at Waikiki. As we approached Oahu, Lieutenant Schick [the unit's medical officer, a passenger] began taking pictures with a small camera he had brought along.

As we passed Diamond Head, I noticed a few bursts of M fire [antiaircraft] across the landmass, off to our right. I thought some American M unit was practising. Then I saw a flight of six pursuit ships [fighter planes] apparently flying through a bunch of ack-ack bursts. I recall thinking that somebody on the ground was getting a little careless about where he was shooting.

It was 08:00. I remember the exact time, because I had to fill out a status report on our engines every hour on the hour.

The after-action record on the *Akagi* states that the strafing of Hickam airfield began at 0800 local time. Hirano's flight probably spotted Reid's B-17 as it made its way along the south shore of Oahu heading towards Hickam. Reid tells the story compellingly.

My status report took a few minutes. When I again looked up, we were on a long base leg to Hickam Field. This leg took us right down the canal toward Pearl Harbor. Captain Swenson ordered me to lower the landing gear. As I did, I noticed a great deal of black smoke coming up from Pearl Harbor. There was too much ack-ack around, and I began to feel that something was wrong, although I still had no idea what it was.

I asked Captain Swenson about the smoke. He thought the islanders were burning sugarcane as he had seen them do during the last trip he made to the islands. I didn't feel too confident about that explanation because I couldn't picture burning sugarcane making such black, oily smoke. In addition, that explanation didn't account for all the shooting. We had made the flight under radio silence, but we were cleared to contact the tower. They had not answered any of our calls. We had to continue our approach; our gas supply would soon become a problem. We were now at 600 feet and turned to our final approach. I got my first clear look at Hickam Field.

What I saw shocked me. At least six planes were burning fiercely on the ground. Gone was any doubt in my mind as to what had happened. Unbelievable as it seemed, I knew we were now in a war! As if to dispel any lingering doubts, two Japanese fighters came from our rear and opened fire.

There were in fact three Zeros attacking one unarmed bomber in the vulnerable position of being about to land – Hirano and his two wingmen.

A tremendous stream of tracer bullets poured by our wings and began to ricochet inside the ship. It began to look as though I would probably have the dubious distinction of being aboard the first Army ship shot down.

Without waiting for an order from Captain Swenson, I pushed the throttles full on, gave it full RPM, and flicked the 'up' switch on the landing gear. It seemed only logical to get quickly into some nearby clouds and try to escape almost certain destruction, since we had no way of fighting back.

Last briefing: Japanese pilots, wearing lifejackets, gather round before take-off

I had no sooner taken these steps than smoke began to pour into the cockpit. The smoke was caused by some of their tracer bullets hitting our pyrotechnics, which were stored amidships. Captain Swenson and I both realized there was now no choice but to try to land. The captain yanked the throttles off, and I popped the landing gear switch to the down position again. The wheels had only come up about halfway, and they came down and locked before we hit the ground. While all this was happening, Lieutenant Schick, who had been standing between Captain Swenson and me, said in disbelief, 'They are shooting at us from the ground.' I had just time to yell at him that the shots came from the back when he screamed that he had been hit in the leg.

Seconds later, we hit the ground. Because of the smoke inside the cockpit, we couldn't see outside very well, and the plane bounced hard. It took both of us on the controls to get the wings level after that first bounce. Then the tail came down. Almost immediately, the plane began to buckle and collapse, breaking in the middle where the fire had burned through. When that happened, we stopped very quickly.

The cockpit was now completely black with smoke, and it was imperative to get out fast. I felt my way back to the top escape hatch and could make out the figure of Captain Swenson as he pulled himself up and out. The plane was in a very awkward position. The rear half, for all intents and purposes, was no longer with us, so when I jumped from the leading edge of the wing, normally about six feet off the ground, I dropped about ten feet [because the rear half was missing and the remaining plane tilted more]. I felt no shock or pain when I landed.

Burnt out: This B-17 has completely lost its tail section

Obeying my first impulse to get away from the ship before it blew up, I ran a few feet forward and came out of the smoke just in time to see a Japanese plane making another pass at us down the runway. I decided it was better to risk blowing up with the plane than to chance getting hit by a Japanese bullet. I ran back to our ship and hopped up on the left tire under the engine nacelle where, I figured, the mass of metal would protect me from the bullets. As soon as I heard the roar of the fighter passing overhead, I dove out of the smoke and looked around.

I spotted Captain Swenson and Lieutenant Taylor but saw none of the others. I guessed that they had already run for the safety of the row of hangars. I later learned, however, that Aviation Cadet Beale had been shot in the leg. Lieutenant Schick, who had been hit once while in the plane, had managed to get out, but a bullet fired from a Japanese plane had struck him in the head.

The three Zeros, then the six in the rest of the flight, turned around and methodically strafed the aircraft in front of the hangars and anyone moving on the airfield. Hirano, in his Zero AI-154, had spotted the figure of the doctor, Lt Schick running as best he could with his leg wound. Hirano, fixated on killing Lt. Schick with his fixed machine guns, had hit the ground, scraping off his belly tank, and bending the propeller blade tips.

Then, while struggling to regain control of his faltering fighter which bounced upwards, then headed in the direction of Fort Kamehameha at extremely low altitude.

The pilot of the Zero behind Hirano recalled (after the war):

He had apparently pulled out too late. His propeller scraped the runway, becoming all twisted. Unable to fly, he zoomed upward with momentum then dove [to crash].

Another eye-witness to these events was a young U.S. Navy PBY pilot, Ensign Harvey N. Hop, newly-wed to Miriam, the daughter of a U.S. Army Warrant Officer. Ensign Hop and Miriam were living with Miriam's father and mother in officers' quarters at Fort Kamehameha, just beyond the Hickam Field fence. Ensign Hop was probably the last surviving person recorded to have seen Hirano alive. Hop later related:

I awoke Sunday, December 7th, to the sound of loud, vibrating explosions. Going to the window of our quarters in Ft. Kamehameha, which overlooked the approach to runway No 5 at Hickam Field, I observed large columns of smoke rising from what appeared to be the Pearl Harbor fuel storage tank areas. ...

As I watched the columns of smoke become more ominous, I saw an aircraft flying west to east diving down over the Hickam hangars.

When an object fell from the plane and exploded in the hangar area I was astounded, but not nearly as much as when the plane banked to head back East and I saw two big red circles on the wing tips. Other single-engine aircraft followed the original one. ...

While still watching the bombing of Hickam Field, we [also] saw a flight of four-engine bombers to the N.E. coming in on an apparent run on Hickam. I thought, 'My God. They have four-engine bombers. Where are they coming from?'

Shortly, I realized the planes were B-17s with a new camouflage paint job and a modified tail, trying to land at Hickam. One landed with a Japanese plane on his rear end and was set on fire as he touched down. The other bombers pulled up and went around. ...

While Miriam and I watched this unbelievable sight, I was getting into my uniform (as) I knew I had to report to my squadron.

Suddenly a Jap plane was hit. As it headed back toward the ocean, we could see the goggled pilot frantically trying to restart his engine. We knew he had to crash and Miriam screamed at me, 'Go kill him! Go kill him!' Later we learned that the Jap plane had crashed into a building a block away and (the crash) had killed several soldiers that were watching the action and were too stunned to move as the plane bore down on them.

Hirano was not, in fact, hit, as James Lansdale's account makes crystal clear.

PO1c Takashi Hirano, flying his Akagai-based Zero, [AI-154], would have felt his belly tank striking the ground while strafing at Hickam Field, and then being ripped off. He would also have felt the impact of propeller blades digging into the runway surface. Out of balance and bent, the propeller blades would have induced a severe vibration of the engine and damage to the engine mounts. Hirano must have struggled to remain airborne a few feet off the ground, as he headed in a west to southwesterly direction toward Fort Kamehameha.

The Zero hit two palm trees in front of the Fort's Machine Shop, where a group of soldiers from C Battery, 41st Coast Artillery Regiment had gathered to watch what was happening. The plane's engine and forward fuselage went in one direction, having hit one tree, as the rest of the plane hit the second tree. Part of the tree trunk was rammed into the cockpit area, instantly killing Hirano. The engine flew off, completely separated, and the rear fuselage was broken in half and twisted round at right angles to the forward section. The men standing watching in disbelief had no chance to get out of the way, as the engine with its bent propellers mowed them down. Four men were killed.

The C.O. of the 1st Battalion, 55th Coast Artillery, Col. William J. McCarthy, who was hurrying past to man his guns at Ahua Point, came across the terrible scene where Hirano's Zero had crashed. He stated:

A Japanese plane had just struck a tree and caromed off the first tree and struck into a wall at my right at the ordnance machine gun shed. That plane was on the ground. The pilot was dead ...stuffed in (by) the tree. In caroming off he struck several men who were in the road. One man was completely decapitated. Another man apparently (had) been hit by the prop, because his legs and arms and head were off, lying right on the grass. The pilot was dead, as I said, in the plane.

Folded in half: Hirano's Zero where its murderous flight ended

12 The chaotic defence

AMERICAN anti-aircraft fire was ineffective and chaotic. One gunner started firing off huge shells from a battleship's turrets, useless against aircraft, only to discover later that he had demolished a block of apartments, killing his own fiancée. Or so an ex-serviceman on Maui told me – I cannot find corroboration of the fiancée detail, but can find an apartment block being destroyed by shellfire, not bombing.

Three civilian workers at Pearl Harbor, rushing to help the Navy, were certainly killed when a shell exploded right over their 1937 Packard Sedan, ironically outside the Japanese consulate. All the damage to Honolulu wreaked by U.S. gunfire was thought at the time to be caused by ruthless Japanese bombing. That is why the first wave – when U.S. guns were unmanned – caused little civilian damage but the second wave much more. Fifteen civilians were killed and many more injured. On the other hand, a few Japanese planes were downed.

A civilian car lies wrecked on Judd Street. This was published as a car destroyed by Japanese bombs. In fact an American anti-aircraft had exploded above it, and such 'friendly fire' did most of the damage to Honolulu

13 The feeble response in the air

THE vast number of aircraft available to the U.S. side – around 400 – made hardly any useful contribution to the fight. Most were parked in the worst possible way – in tight rows, ideal for bombing and strafing, and so close that fuel and munitions fires could spread from one plane to another. There were a few individuals who took off and indeed fought valiantly, but they were a handful. Two heroic men – George Welch and Ken Taylor – who had been up all night playing poker, rushed to an airfield on their own initiative and took off in partly armed Kittyhawks, downing at least four enemy planes. But it was a tiny effort from the massive American forces that should have been available.

Some of the American aircraft in the air were the B-17s heading from the mainland (whose expected arrival had caused radar operators to ignore the vast Japanese air fleet). They arrived during the attack and were aghast to be landing through heavy anti-aircraft fire while being attacked from above. They could do nothing to defend themselves or attack the enemy as, due to the length of the flight from the mainland, (they were supposed to refuel and go onto the Philippines) all armament had been removed to reduce weight. Other U.S. planes in the air included civilian flights, which were shot down by the Japanese, and returning U.S. patrol aircraft, which were shot down by 'friendly fire' from the ground.

Some of the few who fought back in the air that day: Kenneth Taylor and George Welch (left) took off on their own initiative in their Kittyhawks

14 The courageous woman flier

THE first American pilot to encounter the Japanese attack head-on in the air that day was a woman – and what a woman she turned out to be! Civilian flight instructor Cornelia Clark Fort went in the history books twice – as the first American pilot to encounter the Japanese air fleet on their murderous mission and later, having felt compelled to join the war effort more directly, she became the first American female pilot to die doing her duty.

On that fateful morning of December 7, Cornelia (pictured next page) – that then very rare thing, a woman flying instructor, and one who was a very attractive 22-year-old too – took off from John Rodgers civilian airport near the mouth of Pearl Harbor with a male Hawaiian defence worker at 7am for a lesson practising take-offs and landings in an Interstate Cadet monoplane.

After several 'goes round', at 7.45am their plane was lining up for another landing when they saw another plane heading towards them from the far end of the field. She assumed it was an Army Air

Corps pilot cheekily disobeying orders to stay clear of this airfield and goofing around. She ignored it and concentrated on getting her student to land the plane safely.

Cornelia Clark Fort: Deep passion for flying

She looked up from the controls to see the other plane heading straight for them as if for a head-on collision. Just in time, she grabbed the controls and pulled them up sharply. She was astonished to see the other plane pass only feet beneath them, so close the plane was buffeted in the slipstream, and even more amazed to see the 'red balls', as she later put it, on the other plane's wing. She knew what they stood for – the Japanese rising sun – and looking around could see smoke rising and bombs exploding.

Bullets whizzed past as they continued the landing, under her control, followed by another civilian small plane flown by airport manager Bob Tyce.

Cornelia and her pupil ran for cover in the airport hangar, where airport workers expressed disbelief until another man rushed in and said Tyce was dying in a pool of blood on the runway, having been machine-gunned by a strafing plane as he got out of his aircraft.

Cornelia somehow survived the Day of Infamy, perhaps thanks to that first Japanese pilot's poor aim. But there was no more civilian flying allowed in Hawaii as the islands went on a war footing. What could she do?

She was determined to do something for the war effort, and talked her way on to a ship heading for the mainland. She arrived in San Francisco on March 1, 1942, and became something of a celebrity, raising money for war bonds and appearing in a promotional film, plus giving talks on women becoming flyers. But this was, of course, many decades before it was considered that women could become combat flyers, so she knew she could not be a serving fighter or bomber pilot.

But how did a girl come to be a pilot at all in that day and age?

Cornelia was born in 1919, in Nashville, Tennessee to a well-off family. Her father was one of the bosses and owners of the National Life and Accident Insurance Company, so they lived in a mansion on a vast estate where the growing girl could enjoy her passion for horse-riding.

But her father – because of his work in insurance – had a serious worry. He called his three sons together and made them swear on the Bible that they would never fly. In those days it was still a perilous, experimental means of transport. He didn't bother to make Cornelia take the vow – she was only five years old. And why would a girl fly anyway? It was almost unthinkable.

A conventional middle-class childhood followed, and one can see it ending with college education, a nice job like schoolteacher – not that she would need the money – marriage, children and of course more horses. But one day a friend invited Cornelia for a plane ride to Berryfield, Nashville Airport (which is why you will have BNA on your ticket if you ever fly to the modern airport of a different name at that city). That changed her life for ever.

Cornelia loved it so much that she signed up for flying lessons on the spot. Knowing of her brothers' prohibition from flying, she kept quiet at home about her new passion.

Her flight instructor had a simple test for all aspiring pilots. He took them up in an open Interstate Cadet plane, flipped it over, then watched his upside-down students' reactions. If they screamed in panic, it was the end of their hopes. But when he turned to look at Cornelia, she was grinning from ear to ear.

By 1940, with her father dead, Cornelia needed to keep her flying secret no longer, and by summer of that year she became the first woman pilot in Nashville to have a pilot's licence. By March 1941, she was even an instructor.

Cornelia Fort, second left, with women pilots two weeks before she was killed

By September Cornelia, by now brilliant at aerobatics, got that job with Andrews Flying Service at John Rodgers Airfield in Honolulu, Hawaii. War seemed to be coming, but little did she know that by moving to idyllic Hawaii she would end up at the front line of the very first battle of involving the USA.

After her return to the mainland, following her miraculous survival of the Pearl Harbor attack, she initially supported the war effort with talks and lectures. But on September 6, 1942, an offer came that gave her a much more exciting chance. It was from the Women's Auxiliary Ferrying Squadron (WAFS) – the outfit that later became the better-known Women's Airforce Service Pilots (WASP).

The authorities were running short of ready-trained male pilots as they were quickly sent for combat duties, and the service needed ferry pilots to take new aircraft from the factories to airbases where they were needed. So the WAFS was writing to known civilian pilots of all descriptions – women included.

Signed up: Cornelia Fort's permit to fly military aircraft

Delighted, Cornelia did not hesitate and in fact wanted to be to be the first to sign up, setting out by railroad to cross the States to New Castle Army Air Force Base in Wilmington, Delaware. However, another woman flew there in her own plane – it was a pre-war hobby for the well-to-do, remember – making Cornelia the *second* woman to join the WAFS. The women were paid less

A Vultee BT-13 Valiant, similar to the one Cornelia died in

than their male counterparts, and given longer training as if they were somehow more stupid – a bit of an insult as Cornelia was, remember, a top instructor in civilian life. But she shrugged that off and got on with it to get back in the air again as soon as she could.

Yet it ended in tragedy. Stationed at the 6th Ferrying Group base at Long Beach, California, Cornelia Fort became the first WAFS fatality on March 21, 1943 when another plane being flown by a male pilot struck the port wing of the Vultee Valiant BT-13 trainer she was ferrying in mid-air ten miles south of Merkel, Texas.

At the time of the accident, Cornelia Fort was one of the best pilots of the WAFS, so it unlikely her error caused the crash. The footstone of her grave (pictured below) is inscribed, 'Killed in the Service of Her Country'.

That was true enough – but how much better an epitaph would be what Cornelia courageously wrote herself when she realised her service might lead to death.

She wrote presciently in a letter to her mother: '*I want no one to grieve for me. I was happiest in the sky, at dawn when the quietness of the air was like a caress, when the noon sun beat down, and at dusk when the sky was drenched with the fading light. Think of me there and remember me.*'

15 The 'superior' Japanese bombs

THE Japanese achieved such a terrible impact at Pearl Harbor because they had superior armour-piercing bombs and used them skilfully with dive bombers, was the 'fact' some
naval commentators gleaned from the attack.

In reality they didn't have superior armour-piercing bombs. They didn't have *any* such bombs, only developing such weapons later in the war. And the things they used instead were
so cumbersome they couldn't be used in dive bombing but were dropped in level flight by 'Kate' bomber aircraft, and were astonishingly badly made and ineffective.

The Japanese Type 99 bomb: Surprisingly bad

Lacking any such bomb for their sneak attack, the Japanese bodged one up using obsolete 16in gun battleship shells. These Type 99 bombs were huge, way too heavy, and carried little explosive – only 50lb in a bombs weighing 1,760lb, and taller than a man.

They turned off some of the thickness of the shell on lathes, to lighten them, and welded fins to the rear. Whether they did this while the explosive was still present is unknown.

'Kate' bomber

Because of the need to drop them from 10,000ft – to get their armour-piercing speed – most missed their targets. Of those that hit, 20 per cent were duds and did not explode at all. One bomb went clean through all the decks of *USS Vestal*, out of the bottom and exploded on the harbour floor.

The *Vestal* survived the battle to serve on in a long career as a repair ship. More infamously, one of the armour-piercing bombs hit the *USS Arizona*, moored alongside the *Vestal* – which was herself burning from several smaller bombs – and penetrated the ship's magazine before exploding, blowing the battleship almost in half, killing hundreds of men.

The USS Vestal: Lucky escape amidst the massacre

Ironically this blew out *Vestal's* fires. Those sailors who had jumped overboard on an 'abandon ship' order soon realised this had been countermanded, got back on board and manned the ship. Mooring lines were cut with axes and the ship sailed away from the spreading sea of fire around *Arizona's* wreck.

In a strange kind of way the *Vestal* was saved by the Type 99 bomb, twice. By the unreliability of the one that passed clean through her. And by having her raging deck fires blown out by the one that blew up the poor *Arizona*.

First coverage: The American press gave a roughly correct first account, but British newspapers (below) were pretty hopeless to start with

16 The hopeless first reports

THE censorship and the desire of British and American correspondents to do everything to help the Allied war effort meant that reporting was far from accurate. The British *Daily Express* first trumpeted Pearl Harbor as a partial American victory: NAVY BATTLE IN PACIFIC: JAP PLANE CARRIER SUNK. U.S. BATTLESHIP ABLAZE it reported on December 8 with an account of a sea battle with a Japanese fleet 'just off Pearl Harbour'. You know that saying about journalism being 'the first rough draft of history'? Very rough in this case.

17 They'll be sorry!

THE rival *Daily Mail*, to be fair, wasn't much luckier. On the same day, a report was carried which described Pearl Harbor as 'one of the most strongly fortified naval bases in the world'. It went on 'Japanese, trying an assault on Pearl Harbour, will certainly meet trouble'. Well I suppose that was true, in the long run. Not on the day, though. The Japanese were pretty pleased with themselves.

18 Ordeal of the trapped men

WHEN the bombed battleship *West Virginia* was raised in 1944, salvage officers found a storeroom calendar with the dates crossed off until December 23, 1941 - 16 days after the ship was sunk. Three men had lived that long in an air pocket using emergency rations. Some sailors had knocked on the upturned ship's bottoms where they had been trapped and at least one was rescued by men with cutting torches, but sadly not these three.

19 The key missed targets

FOR an attack that was supposedly so totally devastating and involved 360 aircraft in several waves, it's surprising that the Japanese failed to hit the very clearly visible oil tanks, lifeblood of the American fleet, and didn't sink any aircraft carrier (out at sea on the day), the ships that soon started the naval defeat of the Japanese at Midway. Or damage the submarine base. This ensured their eventual defeat.

20 The forgotten invasion of Hawaii

THERE *was* an invasion of Hawaii during the Pearl Harbor attacks. Pilots had been told if they could not continue in damaged planes to crash-land on an uninhabited island called Ni'ihau. A submarine would, they were assured, pick them up from there. This is what happened to Shigenori Nishikaichi who landed his crippled Zero fighter on the island. In fact several native Hawaiians lived there and rescued the dazed pilot from his upended plane, having the presence of mind to remove his papers and pistol while they could. They had no knowledge of the war having started, thinking the crash was merely an accident, so laid on a traditional welcoming party for their unexpected guest.

Meanwhile one of the ethnic Japanese families who lived there, told secretly - in their own language, that is - of the attack on Pearl Harbor and the start of the war, changed sides and found weapons to help with the takeover of the island. The native Hawaiians refused even under death threats to return the secret papers and pistol, while one man made a journey to the next island to raise the alarm (there was no radio or telephone communication to Ni'ihau).

In a struggle with firearms, the pilot was killed and one Hawaiian injured. As the takeover of the island failed, one of the Japanese residents committed suicide and the other family were arrested. Interestingly, despite liberals' enthusiasm to present the internment of ethnic Japanese during World War II as some awful, shameful racist impulse, this incident shows that given the chance – and attacks on California were being considered – at least some Japanese could change sides very readily, while it is true that a great many others loyally aided the U.S. war effort.

21 The 'help' it rendered the U.S. Navy

THE assumption that the loss or damage of several battleships crippled the U.S. Navy's prosecution of the war against Japan is an error. It *improved* it to a certain degree. During the war, all the major navies were finding out to their horror that battleships were massively vulnerable to air and submarine attack, with horrendous losses each time in terms of men and expensive resources – whereas subs and planes were way, way smaller, cheaper and quicker to build. (The Italians had lost most of theirs; the British were deeply shocked at the loss of two of their most powerful battleships to Japanese planes, a few days after this; Hitler in the end despaired of his highly-advanced surface fleet ever achieving much as the big ships were lost to the British one after the other; and the Japanese built the biggest battleship in history but it was sunk almost on its first mission). No, the Japanese left the U.S. Navy with no choice but to concentrate on aircraft carriers and submarines – the very weapons that worked in the new naval warfare. These ensured the steady defeat of Japanese empire-building, the crippling of Japanese industry and the near starvation of the people.

22 FDR's 'Day of infamy' speech

PRESIDENT F.D. Roosevelt's speech to Congress the following day is known as the 'Day of infamy speech' – but he didn't ever say that exact phrase. (This is less pedantically petty than the type of discussion which goes 'Did Clint Eastwood ever say: "Do you feel

DRAFT No. 1   December 7, 1941.

PROPOSED MESSAGE TO THE CONGRESS

Yesterday, December 7, 1941, a date which will live in ~~world history~~ *infamy*,

the United States of America was ~~simultaneously~~ *suddenly* and deliberately attacked

by naval and air forces of the Empire of Japan.

The United States was at the moment at peace with that nation and was

~~continuing the~~ *still in* conversation with its Government and its Emperor looking

toward the maintenance of peace in the Pacific. Indeed, one hour after

Japanese air squadrons had commenced bombing in ~~Hawaii and the Philippines~~ *Oahu*

the Japanese Ambassador to the United States and his colleague delivered

to the Secretary of State a formal reply to a ~~former~~ *recent American* message. ~~from the~~

~~Secretary.~~ *While* This reply ~~contained a statement~~ *stated* that diplomatic negotiations

~~must be considered at an end, but~~ *it* contained no threat ~~and no~~ *or* hint of ~~an~~ *war*

armed attack.

It will be recorded that the distance ~~of Manila, and especially~~ of

Hawaii from Japan make*s* it obvious that the~~y~~ attack ~~were~~ *was* deliberately

planned many days ago. During the intervening time the Japanese Govern-

ment has deliberately sought to deceive the United States by false

statements and expressions of hope for continued peace.

lucky, punk?" in the movie – he didn't – because this was real history being made and shows how FDR was reacting, and reacting better than, you might think, George W. Bush on 9/11). In fact the word 'infamy' didn't even appear in his first typed draft which started: 'Yesterday, December 7, 1941, a date which will live in world history, the United States of America was simultaneously and deliberately attacked by naval and air forces of the Empire of Japan.'

The words 'world history' were scratched out in pencil by the President and 'infamy' written over them. At the end of the sentence, he added 'without warning', then changed his mind and crossed that out and changed 'simultaneously' to 'suddenly'. The President is pictured making the speech (left), his son James in uniform to the right.

Much of the speech points out that Japan must have been planning and starting the attack while making peace negotiations with the USA – and this deception was what FDR wanted to impress on the world and his own people: the righteous anger of an innocent victim of aggression, reluctantly forced into war. He'd wanted to fight alongside Churchill, but isolationists prevented him. Now he had cast-iron authority at last.

23 The 'army' of Japanese on Hawaii

WHILE the Pacific war raged on two years after Pearl Harbor, Hawaii was swarming with 150,000 Japanese who lived there and were most mostly unhelpful to Japanese spies. But a visiting *Daily Mail* writer commented: 'Imagine how concerned we would be if we had 150,000 people of German stock milling around Scapa Flow.' It's a similar key naval anchorage in the Orkney Islands, north of Scotland.

24 The crackpot conspiracy theories

THERE have been almost as many conspiracy theories about Pearl Harbor as about President Kennedy's assassination. One author, John Toland, said President Roosevelt was so eager to get America into the war that although he knew of the coming attack, he did nothing to warn the naval commanders at Pearl Harbor. But the idea that a U.S. president would deliberately sacrifice thousands of American lives and capital ships has been shot down in flames by most serious historians. Massive local incompetence is more likely to blame for the poor alertness and feeble response.

Shattering: The moment the magazine in USS Shaw blew up, caught on film

Got him: A rare picture of a Japanese attacker being shot down

USS California slowly sinking after suffering huge bomb and torpedo damage

Ships which didn't sink immediately suffered uncontrollable raging fires

Stunned: Sailors at the air station on Ford Island watch USS Shaw blow up

Missed target: The oil tanks at Pearl Harbor were hardly well camouflaged

News spreads: If the Japanese thought Americans would be knocked out of the war, they miscalculated. They were soon queueing to join the fight

Recruiting and war bonds posters – note the Japanese offering America the olive branch at the same time as stabbing her in the back

25 Did Churchill know and keep quiet?

ANOTHER conspiracy theory says British PM Winston Churchill knew of the attack but didn't tell the Americans, to force them into the war. One problem with this – as with the claim that he let defenceless Coventry be blitzed rather than compromise intelligence sources - is that it can't be proved and Winston can't sue. Another one is that if he knew all the Japanese plans, why was he so utterly appalled that two British battleships the *Prince of Wales* and *Repulse* were sunk by them two days later? Churchill recalled later:

'In all the war I never received a more direct shock. As I turned and twisted in bed the full horror of the news sank in upon me. There were no British or American capital ships in the Indian Ocean or the Pacific except the American survivors of Pearl Harbor who were hastening back to California.'

If there had been a conspiracy, it seems unlikely that the truth would not have come out by now, but even if he had known, would the United Kingdom fighting on alone (with her empire) and hypothetically knowing in advance of the Pearl Harbor plans have been wise to let the Japanese attack? Probably yes, but a couple of hours' warning might have helped the defenders (had they taken any notice!). That's what makes conspiracy theories believable – they kind of make sense. But it doesn't make them fact.

26 Admiral Kimmel's immediate shame

ADMIRAL Husband E. Kimmel (pictured) was in charge of the U.S. Navy Pacific Fleet at Pearl Harbor (although not of the ground-based defence). He watched in horror from the window of his office, and the extent to which he took immediate, deep personal blame was

evident. As Edwin Layton recalled: 'Kimmel stood by the window of his office at the submarine base, his jaw set in stony anguish. As he watched the disaster across the harbor unfold with terrible fury, a spent .50 caliber machine gun bullet crashed through the glass. It brushed the admiral before it clanged to the floor. It cut his white jacket and raised a welt on his chest. "It would have been merciful had it killed me," Kimmel murmured to his communications officer, Commander Maurice "Germany" Curts.'

And another serviceman — who had also been alongside Admiral Kimmel during the attack — told the British *World At War* TV series 30 years later that as Kimmel watched the destruction of the fleet, he tore off his four-star shoulder boards, in apparent recognition of the impending end of his command.

Nor was it the end of his misery. Kimmel lost his son Manning, when a U.S. submarine was sunk in the Philippines in 1944. A handful of men including Manning managed to scramble off the mined vessel as it sank; they were 'rescued' by the Japanese, dried out, interrogated, then put in a ditch, doused with petrol and burned alive. That's the sort of enemy the Allies faced.

So was Admiral Kimmel totally to blame?

27 U.S. Intelligence: 'Magic' became tragic

The U.S. Navy and the Washington Intelligence chiefs had plenty of chances to understand what was about to happen, and in fact clear warnings of when and how it would. The prevailing view, remember, had been that the relative shallowness of Pearl Harbor made air-dropped torpedoes useless. However, after the British strike at Taranto (see item 5), this became in doubt and the U.S. Navy requested a chart of that harbour, marked with depths, which proved that it *was* possible. This is in the Navy archives in Washington, but no one showed then to Admiral Kimmel, in charge at Hawaii, the harbour most at risk from this type of attack.

This was **Glaringly Obvious Clue No 1**. Kimmel was left thinking that the safest place to keep his fleet was Pearl Harbor, when it was the most dangerous place.

Glaringly Obvious Clue No 2 was that a double agent called Popov had intercepted a message between Tokio and Berlin. In this, the Japanese had asked for any information about precise depths at Pearl Harbor and whether there were anti-torpedo nets in place. This information, which all but announced Japan's precise intention, was shown to the FBI and its director Edgar Hoover. Yet again, no one told Kimmel. Hoover was more interested in being morally censorious about Popov's James Bond-like sexual conquests.

Glaringly Obvious Clue No 3 was an intercepted message – using the USA's brilliant and top secret decoding systems known as 'Magic' – from Tokio to the Japanese consulate in Hawaii asking what ships were in Pearl Harbor and to plot their positions on a grid, and to report this twice a week. This was read in Washington, and yet again, astonishingly, even though this U.S. Navy information was passed secretly to Winston Churchill, no one told their own admiral in Hawaii. Astonishing. The nickname 'Magic' was said to have been given to the decoding system by Roosevelt because of the fact that he could read the enemy's most secret messages before the intended recipient had even decoded them!

Glaringly Obvious Clue No 4: Messages were intercepted from Tokio to its embassy in Washington about the supposed peace talks taking place. They said it was no use changing things after November 25. Things would be 'unstoppable' after that. Why would that be? Well, an examination of the previous Glaringly Obvious Clues made it pretty clear. That would the date the fleet would sail from Japan, and maintaining strict radio silence, it would be difficult to call them back.

Glaringly Obvious Clue No 5. On the day there was the famous 14-part coded message from Tokio to the Japanese Embassy and its 'peace negotiation' team in Washington. This slowly made it clear – only by the 14th part – that war was to start, without actually declaring it. It said to break off talks and destroy decoding machines and code books at exactly noon Washington time – as an Intelligence officer realised at the time: 'You only say this when you are about to start hostilities, and this precise time of noon, we pretty quickly realised, was 7.30am in Hawaii on a Sunday morning, ideal time for an attack'. Because of decoding problems at the Japanese Embassy, the Americans had this vital information first. It was like playing poker not only having a mirror behind your opponent's hand, but even being told what cards he would be dealt next – *if* the information was passed to those who actually needed it. So what was done to use this great advantage?

This information was rushed to the White House and to Admiral Harold Stark, Chief of Naval Operations. The Intelligence officer assumed Hawaii would be urgently told. Amazingly, nothing was done.

As Kimmel's grandson said recently, imagine what difference

such a warning would have made. Anti-aircraft guns all manned, radar on proper alert, ships steaming out of the Harbor, fighter aircraft on patrol ready to strike, maybe even a revenge strike on the vulnerable aircraft carriers – they could have given Japan a bloody nose there and then instead of waiting for the Battle of Midway to do that. In the end, it was realised that nothing had been done with just 70 minutes left to the first wave arriving over Pearl Harbor. It still would have been enough to change the story.

Anti-aircraft shells burst above burning ships during the second wave attack

The military frantically tried to radio Hawaii – but atmospheric conditions were bad and they could not make contact. They then sent a telegram. This warning was not marked with the correct priority, so was kept in the telegraph office on Hawaii until the raid had finished, then delivered afterwards by bicycle – eight hours too late!

Given all this staggering incompetence in Washington, which was again and again given clear indications of Japanese intentions, in terms of where, when and how the attack would come, it was a little unfair – if rather convenient – to load all the blame for the dismal performance of the U.S. forces at Hawaii on Kimmel, who became the scapegoat during the war and was quickly relieved of his command and demoted. Only at Congressional hearings after the war did it start to become clear that Washington was equally to blame.

It was hard to explain why this was, but one suggestion was that secrecy inside Washington was too good, to the point of making intelligence worthless. When Magic intelligence was received, no one was allowed to keep the papers. They were circulated by an officer with a guarded, locked brief case who waited while the President, or Secretary for the Navy, or whoever, looked at the sheet of paper, then they were taken away. No copies, notes, or photographs were allowed. This was great for security, and the Japanese never found out that their every move was known about in advance. But no one in Washington could ever look at all the papers together and form an overall picture.

This still cannot explain the unbelievable, culpable inaction close to the day itself. It was an ocean-going national scandal.

28 The forgotten second raid on Pearl

THERE was – which fact surprises most people – a second Japanese air raid on Pearl Harbor, three months later. The Japanese knew they had missed the oil storage depots which fuelled American operations in the Pacific, and they also wanted to disrupt the salvage efforts, aiming to raise some of the sunken warships to carry the fight to the Japanese. They also needed to make a reconnaissance – where were the potentially highly dangerous American aircraft carriers? The reason that few of us have heard of it that it was an abject failure.

By this time Japanese forces could not approach nearly so near, so five very long-range flying boats – huge planes with 124ft wingspan – were assigned for the Operation K mission, the longest bombing raid in history at the time. Nicknamed 'Flying Porcupines' by the Allies, these planes possessed not only an amazing 24hr-hour endurance but also bristled with ten machine-guns and ten cannon.

The huge Emily class flying boat, nicknamed 'the Flying Porcupine'

On the day, March 4, 1942, only two of the planes were

serviceable, and took off from the Marshall islands. They had a secret refueling rendezvous with a submarine at French Frigate Shoal. When they at last arrived at Hawaii, the weather was appalling, luckily for the Americans. One of the planes glimpsed Tantalus Peak on Oahu at about 2am, and dropped his bombs on Roosevelt High School (they missed). The second plane tried to bomb Pearl Harbor but hit the sea outside. The cloud combined with an effective blackout made any reconnaissance impossible.

This time, of course, the island's air defence was alert, the planes were spotted on radar and searchlight and anti-aircraft guns manned, and fighter aircraft took off. But nothing could be done in the cloud and the giant Japanese planes lumbered off home, their mission a total failure. The Japanese press claimed damage at Pearl Harbour, with 30 deaths, but the reality was two windows had been broken at an empty high school.

An attempted third operation on March 10 ended with the 'Flying Porcupine' being shot down near Midway Atoll. Crucially, after this the Imperial Japanese Navy had no direct way of observing American naval movements.

29 Hitting back with broomsticks

EVERYONE knows that ultimately, Pearl Harbor in December 1941 led to two flights dropping atom bombs on Japan in August 1945. They sowed the wind and reaped a terrible whirlwind.

Less well known are the two earlier revenge raids, and utterly astonishing ones they were too. The first was the one where broomsticks were used as defence. But it worked.

The Doolittle Raid, coming just four months after Pearl Harbor, was an apparently impossible attack on Tokio by U.S. bombers. On Saturday, April 18, 1942, the raid was a massive blow to the Japanese, who thought they were invulnerable, as they had shattered American military might and pushed them back across the enormous Pacific towards their own shores. People in Tokio felt safe, far from any possible action.

They might after the raid have begun to suspect it wasn't going to be a glorious and quick victory after all. Just how much the opposite would become clearer over the next two years.

It was also a brilliant boost to damaged American morale, and gave U.S. troops all around the Pacific theatre more confidence in President Roosevelt's key sentence in his 'Infamy' speech:

'No matter how long it may take us to overcome this premeditated invasion, the American people in their righteous might will win through to absolute victory.'

But good God, it was courageous! Few of the men expected to return, and they knew their aircraft could not make it back to their carriers. A total of 15 of the 16 bombers failed to return; that only 11 of the 80 airmen involved were lost was, frankly, a good outcome given the near-suicidal plan.

It was named after Lieutenant Colonel James 'Jimmy' Doolittle of the United States Army Air Forces, (pictured) who led it. After practising on a runway painted with a silhouette of an aircraft carrier deck, it had been realised that a twin-engined medium bomber, not designed for naval warfare, could take off from such a deck.

The aircraft chosen was the B-25 Mitchell. At a civilian airline base in the Midwest, closely guarded and shrouded in secrecy, the B-25s were heavily modified, having one gun turret removed to save weight, and the rear turret fitted with dummy broom-handle guns. Only the top turret and one forward gun remained operational. Extra fuel tanks were installed, and the heavy bomb sight replaced with a lightweight one. Not only would the raiders lack the usual fighter protection, but they would have few guns to protect themselves.

Volunteers for an unspecified 'dangerous mission' stepped forward in the chosen bomber group. Training took place in Florida, to avoid any hint that an early attack on Japan was dreamed of.

The aircraft were loaded on the *USS Hornet* on April 1, 1942, near San Francisco and met a task force off Hawaii a few days later. The powerful force comprised two carriers, three heavy cruisers, one light cruiser, eight destroyers and two fleet oilers. Eventually, the slower vessels

withdrew, leaving the carriers and cruiser to dash into enemy-controlled waters near enough to Japan to launch the raid.

Then disaster struck early on the morning of April 17. The American ships were spotted by a small Japanese patrol vessel. That was sunk, but not before the crew had got off a radio warning. The American commanders now knew they could be attacked from the mainland or by sea within a few hours, and one of the carriers had its decks blocked by the B-25s, so launching its fighters was impossible.

The decision was made to launch immediately, although they were 170 miles further away from the targets than planned.

The first plane had just 142 metres in which to take off. None of the pilots had taken off from a carrier before. Yet all 16 got airborne.

The raid's B-25s packed tightly on the deck of the USS Hornet

They bombed ten military and industrial targets in Tokio, two in Yokohama and one in each of Osaka, Nagoya and Yokosuka. The idea was as much to spread fear through a wide area as to do any substantial damage to the Japanese war machine. Some 50 Japanese were killed by the four bombs each plane carried and the strafing of targets by the nose gunners. The consequences included more Japanese resources being transferred to homeland defence, and the decision to hurry the ill-fated attack on, and invasion of, the American-held Midway Island, a stepping stone to Hawaii.

There was some light anti-aircraft fire and a few fighter attacks but in general the Japanese were as ill-prepared as the Americans at

Pearl Harbor. Three Japanese aircraft were shot down by the B-25s, and Doolittle noted with some satisfaction that the broom-handle dummy guns in the rear turrets had done a good job – none of his planes was attacked from the rear.

They all left Japan intact, but the rest of the story is grimmer reading. The plan was to head for nearby China.

Some of the aircraft ran out of fuel and the crews had to bail out. One aircraft made it to the Soviet Union, where the aircraft was impounded and the crew interned. Some of those who bailed out in China were captured by the Japanese. Tens of thousands of Chinese were killed during the Japanese army's ruthless revenge sweep of the whole area.

Three crew were killed in action (trying to bail out or crash land); of the eight who were captured by the Japanese, three were executed, one died of diseases and four were eventually freed in a terrible state after being mistreated. One of the men returned to Japan as a missionary after the war, and served there for 30 years.

The rest of the raiders fought on through the rest of the war. They held reunions for many years, turning over the 80 named goblets they'd had made for crew members one by one as they died. At the time of writing, just one remains alive, aged 101.

Doolittle himself believed he would face a court-martial for losing nearly all his aircraft. Instead he was given a Medal of Honor by the President, and promoted two grades straight to General. Doolittle had done a lot.

30 The water pipes that changed history

THE Battle of Midway (June 4-7, 1942), only six months after Pearl Harbor, was one of the two most important naval battles of all time, truly up there with Trafalgar (1815) in its significance. Both conflicts left the victor with a century of naval dominance of the world. At Midway, a Japanese thrust aimed at knocking America out of the war was defeated with all four aircraft carriers plus a heavy cruiser being sunk. It was the turning point of the war, and although there was a bloody conflict ahead, Japan never regained the naval initiative.

But how did the Americans know where to ambush the fleet, secretly heading for Midway Island? They had broken Japanese naval code and knew that a huge operation was being planned against location 'AF', but were not sure where that was. Looking at maps made Midway seem a possible target, so commanders at Hawaii told Midway via secure undersea cable to broadcast a complaint by radio in plain English back to Hawaii that their water supply was broken. It wasn't (unlike the Japanese naval code) but in a salt water-surrounded atoll that could be bad news. Within 24 hours, Japanese naval code was advising their forces that target AF was short of water. Bingo! Now the trap could be set.

31 The costly revenge and design errors

I READ recently how 'American torpedo bombers wreaked a terrible revenge for Pearl Harbor at the Battle of Midway'. It *was* terrible, but tragically not in the way the writer meant.

The torpedo bombers sent from the U.S. carriers were Douglas Devastators, a somewhat obsolete design (below), slow and under-armed, and they arrived before the dive bombers. They were massacred in a turkey shoot, poor beggars.

Of the first wave of 15, all were shot down without causing any damage. Only one crew member survived and he did so by wisely hiding under a floating seat cushion until the battle was over – the Japanese had a way of torturing 'rescued' airmen for information, and then murdering them. The next wave of 14 lost ten, the next wave of 12 lost ten – all without hitting the target, I was going to say – but at least one of the scandalously hopeless American torpedoes (details next item) hit a Japanese ship and bounced off with an audible clang, without exploding. Others ran under the target ships, and some exploded on being dropped into the

water (one being dropped from a Devastator, right).

It looked as if the Japanese were going to win this battle hands-down and the invasion fleet, following behind, could land on Midway. It was the last time these hopeless aircraft were used by the Americans, and it was realised that torpedo design had to be improved (next item). But the men's sacrifice distracted the Japanese from what was to happen next.

In fact, all this time, chaos reigned on the Japanese aircraft carriers, which had launched one air raid on the island of Midway. They had been rearming their reserve force with ground attack bombs because of American air attacks launched from Midway, which had clearly not been put out of action. A second attack there was needed, the Japanese commanders decided.

During the Battle of Midway, one of the islands under fire (diorama)

Then the arrival of the doomed American torpedo planes from a carrier – and the sighting of one carrier by a patrol plane – made the Admiral dither, then order the planes to be rearmed with torpedoes and bombs suitable for attacking ships. While this was going on, Japanese planes were still returning from the first strike on Midway.

A major design flaw of the Japanese aircraft carriers meant that full fuel lines and ammunition piles were all over the places, with no thought for fire control. Other carrier forces knew to drain down fuel lines not in use, and to shield ammunition deep in the magazines.

At that point a Japanese seaman on one of carriers looked skywards. Small black dots were visible. They became plunging American dive bombers. One of the Japanese pilots, Mitsuo Fuchida

A Dauntless releases its deadly payload. Note the dive brakes on the wings

A Dauntless prepares to dive again on the Mikuma, on fire far below

Simply shattered: Last moments of the Japanese cruiser Mikuma

(mentioned above as leading the Pearl Harbor attack), was on the carrier *Akagi* at the time and memorably later described the moment.

'A look-out screamed: "Hell-Divers!" I looked up to see three black enemy planes plummeting towards our ship. Some of our machineguns managed to fire a few frantic bursts at them, but it was too late. The plump silhouettes of the American Dauntless dive-bombers quickly grew larger, and then a number of black objects suddenly floated eerily from their wings.'

One of the American pilots described how the flight deck of one of the carriers peeled open in all directions, revealing the hangar full of aircraft below.

In fact the *Akagi* was hit by only one bomb, and while on U.S. and British aircraft carriers this would have merely hampered operations for a while, it proved fatal because of the fuel lines and stacked munitions mentioned above.

Fires and explosions tore uncontrollably through the ship, aircraft flipping over in the blasts. Eventually all four Japanese aircraft carriers were sunk, and any of their planes in the air had nowhere to go.

Another hit: Trying to repair the Yorktown

One U.S. carrier, the *Yorktown* was also sunk after absorbing a staggering amount of damage several times (the Japanese were sure she had been sunk twice, and they were therefore sinking several carriers, but she was heroically patched up and continued to fight to the last).

The heroic USS Yorktown, patched up so many times, burns fiercely

The balance of the war had shifted, and would not be changed back. Japan had lost four carriers, one heavy cruiser, one destroyer,

248 aircraft and 3,057 killed, many of them with the not easily replaced skills needed to conduct naval air war.

The Americans, by contrast, lost one previously badly damaged aircraft carrier, one destroyer, 150 aircraft and 307 killed. They could and did rapidly build new carriers. The Japanese, increasingly starved of materials by blockading submarines during the rest of the war, could not. Nor could they replace the skilled men they continued to rapidly lose.

The USS Arizona, burning after being hit at Pearl Harbor, about to sink

32 Impossible odds, from Zeros to heroes

THE 'Thach Weave' sounds like something learned in a handcraft class – perhaps rug-making, that kind of thing. Home-spun.

In fact it was desperately needed tactic for the US Navy pilots, devised just before Pearl Harbor, to make the impossible happen.

The faster, tighter turning and faster climbing Japanese fighter, the Mitsubishi A6M 'Zero' that would evidently soon be US pilots' principal enemy, would surely always defeat the slower-turning American Grumman F4F Wildcat fighters, the US Navy's main fighter of the time. Logically, the Zeros would massacre the Wildcats, as they did the obsolete British planes in Malaya.

San Diego-based naval aviator Lt Cdr 'Jimmy' John S. Thach discovered this massive disadvantage US forces would be fighting with from secret Intelligence reports in September 1941. He put his mind to devising a tactic that would defeat the Japanese attackers – one reason the Zeros were so fast and agile was that were flimsily built with little protection for fuel tanks or engine or pilot. If only you could hit them, they would very quickly catch fire. But you had to get into a position to hit them, in a slower plane, the heavily built and harder-to-destroy Wildcat. How could you do that?

The basic Thach Weave notion was of two American fighter aircraft side-by-side. When a Zero attacked one Wildcat, the two Americans turned towards each other. This gave the aircraft not being attacked a chance to sweep the Zero close behind his wingman with raking fire. If this missed, the American aircraft turned towards each other again, and the wingman again would attack the enemy, who had no chance of escaping if he was to continue his attack on the first plane. They would repeatedly cross paths – the 'weave' – until one of the aircraft was destroyed, probably the Japanese one as it could take very few hits and survive, unlike the heavier Wildcat.

To test it, Thach sent up four Wildcats to play the attackers, and four to play the defenders. The defenders had their throttles fixed so they could not reach full power, this mimicking the experience of being attacked by faster aircraft. It worked. One of the attackers, Ensign Edward O'Hare, excitedly told Thach: 'Skipper, it really worked. I couldn't make any attack without seeing the nose of one of your airplanes pointed at me.'

Sadly, as history records, US aircraft at Pearl Harbor a few weeks later were not prepared for the attack and would not have yet known about this new tactical trick. They were mostly destroyed on the ground and the American aircraft carriers – thankfully – were missing.

But by the time of the Battle of Midway, US Navy pilots had been trained. It worked! The slower, less agile fighters were shooting down the faster, tighter-turning Zeros. Thach himself was involved and his wingman, Ensign R. A. M. Dibb, was attacked by a Japanese pilot and turned towards Thach, who dived under his wingman and fired at the incoming enemy aircraft's belly until flames spread along it. Thach's small group of Wildcats took on a much larger force of Zeros and destroyed perhaps half a dozen, while losing just one themselves. Most importantly, the Japanese fighting this battle failed to spot the Dauntless dive bombers that would doom their carriers.

The tactic was also used at the Battle of the Santa Cruz Islands and the battles from Henderson Field on Guadalcanal. The Japanese were perplexed that they could not overcome what they saw as inferior, slower aircraft than the nimble Zero (pictured).

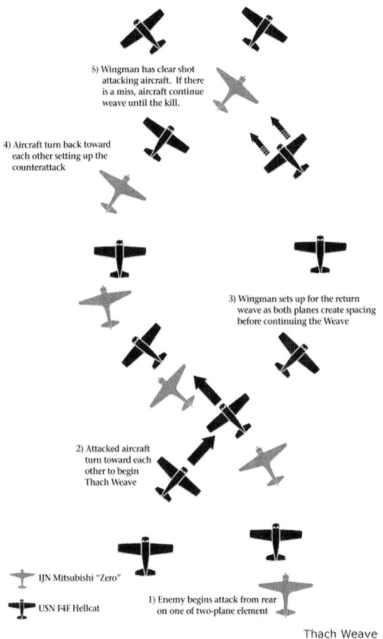

5) Wingman has clear shot attacking aircraft. If there is a miss, aircraft continue weave until the kill.

4) Aircraft turn back toward each other setting up the counterattack

3) Wingman sets up for the return weave as both planes create spacing before continuing the Weave

2) Attacked aircraft turn toward each other to begin Thach Weave

IJN Mitsubishi "Zero"

USN F4F Hellcat

1) Enemy begins attack from rear on one of two-plane element

Thach Weave
Drawn by William S. Smith
Encyclopedia of Arkansas History & Culture

. Those not shot down returned to base furious and humiliated. One Japanese ace recalled after the war: 'For the first time Lt. Commander Tadashi Nakajima encountered what was to become a famous double-team manoeuvre on the part of the enemy. Two Wildcats jumped on the commander's plane. He had no trouble in getting on the tail of an enemy fighter, but never had a chance to fire before the Grumman's team-mate roared at him from the side. Nakajima was raging when he got back to Rabaul; he had been forced to dive and run for safety.'

Lt Cdr John Thach: Brilliant tactic   Picture: US NAVY

Thach's own account of the battle included this: 'Pure logic would convince anyone that with their superior performance and the number of Zeros they were throwing into the fight, we could not possibly survive. "Well," I said, talking to myself, "we're going to take a lot of them with us if they're going to get us all." We kept on working this weave, and it seemed to work better and better. How much time this took, I don't know, but ever since then I haven't the slightest idea how many Zeros I shot down. I just can't remember, and I don't suppose it makes too much difference. It only shows that I was absolutely convinced that nobody could get out of there, that we weren't coming back…'

The Americans would send their experienced pilots back to training schools to impart their experience. The Japanese did not learn quickly from the Thach Weave because their pilots were either dead or hidden in disgrace – the naval authorities covered up their defeats lest the army, who hated them, should find out. New recruits made the same mistakes and fell victim to the Thach Weave too.

Later the problem of dealing with Zeros was dealt with by Grumman's replacement naval fighter, the F6F Hellcat which could catch and beat the Zero one-to-one. Thach retired as an admiral.

33 The scandal beneath the waves

If the Japanese had wanted to sabotage the US Navy's torpedo capability, lessening the threat of revenge after Pearl Harbor, it is doubtful they could have done it more effectively than the Americans did themselves. Their torpedoes and the factories that produced them were stunningly, appallingly awful. I was going to say you might as well have thrown a frozen cod at the enemy, making a similar harmless clang on a ship's hull, but it was worse than that because a frozen cod wouldn't have sunk their own side. And the cost!

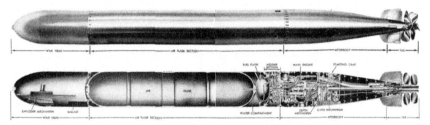

The culprit was the Mark 14 torpedo (pictured) which started its miserable life in 1931 to replace a First World War weapon. In fact that war had been a disaster for U.S. torpedo production – the Navy had almost 300 destroyers each with 12 torpedo tubes, but was sent just 20 when the war started. The Navy then ordered 5,900 of which only about 400 were delivered by the end of the First World War.

You'd think these humiliating lessons would have been heeded between the wars. They weren't. Things just got worse.

In the 1931 effort to produce a better weapon, because ships' anti-torpedo belts were getting more formidable, it was decided to use a top secret Mark 6 Magnetic Influence Exploder. The idea was that a torpedo could run under the target ship and still explode there – where the hull was much thinner – because it sensed the magnetic effect of the ship above it.

This device was so secret that although thousands of running tests were carried out, no live firing was ever run (even though the Navy was offered an old hulk to sink) and the instruction manual's single copy was locked in a safe and never shown to the personnel who need to maintain and operate the damn thing. The Navy thought it too expensive to actually blow up a torpedo in tests, so never did. With catastrophic results.

Yes, torpedoes are complex things to build. In a panic, as the 1930s wore on, the authorities provided more funds and a new factory. Even then as one report states it 'produced only 1½ torpedoes a day in 1937, despite having three shifts of three thousand workers working around the clock'. More factories were brought into the process but it was still woefully bad.

In the first year after the U.S. joined the Second World War, almost as many torpedoes were fired as were produced by three factories working flat out. Perversely, because there was such a shortage, the torpedoes still weren't tested!

In action, they were often useless or worse. They frequently ran under the targets without exploding. They sometimes hit the target square-on with a big clang and didn't go off (this was the other, contact exploder not working – it had been taken from the previous slower torpedo and simply didn't work well at higher speeds; but again no one tested it). The magnetic exploder sometimes worked far too early – so it would explode maybe 100 yards out from the Japanese ship. The submarine commander, watching through the periscope, thought he'd hit the ship. The Japanese, puzzled, just carried on, now using evasive tactics.

The frustration of the courageous American crews must have been immense. For example, on July 9, 1943, *USS Tunny* was in an perfect position to sink three Japanese aircraft carriers. A fantastic contribution to victory if achieved! Seven torpedoes were fired. All seven exploded prematurely, doing no damage. Many such opportunities were missed.

On 24 July 1943, the *USS Tinosa* had at least damaged a Japanese whale factory ship. There were no enemy warships around, so the commander Dan Daspit decided to test out the Mark 14 in textbook fashion. He manoeuvred to the ideal firing position, 800 yards off the stationary target's beam and fired nine torpedoes straight at it. They were *all* duds.

The circular running problem could be tragic. The *USS Tullibee* (pictured) was sunk by one of her own torpedoes on 26 March 1944 while on her fourth patrol. Only one crew member survived – 59 men died.

The explanation of the running too deep problem was so staggering, stupidly simple, it is still embarrassing. As mentioned before, officials were paranoid about wasting a torpedo in the limited running tests they performed. So they fitted them with dummy warheads which floated so they could be sure to retrieve the weapon after the run. When they fired them in combat with heavy warheads on the front, guess what - they ran deeper.

Carefully does it: A torpedo is loaded into a submarine via a deck hatch

Eventually these scandalous defects were finally fixed by a series of modifications. The U.S. Navy was able to strangle Japan's supply route with frequent sinkings of nearly all shipping. The country was starved of food, fuel, raw materials and slave labour. The Mark 14 did its deadly job – at long last. One of the world's worst weapons had become one of its best.

Had the Americans sunk all those juicy Japanese targets at the start of the Pacific War, Japan might have been defeated far more quickly and thousands of Asian civilians and Allied PoWs being abused, tortured, starved and worked to death would have survived. On the other hand, had the Japanese - who started that war with much superior submarines and torpedoes - actually realised what a weapon they had at their disposal, things could have turned out differently. They brilliantly realised that aircraft carriers were one new tool for 'blue water' offensives. They never really grasped that the other one, the submarine, was as important, and like most other navies carried on building battleships, etc, which were rapidly sunk by the other two weapons, a disastrous waste of men and materials.

Thus the biggest battleships ever built – 72,800 tonnes at full load – with the biggest guns ever mounted on a ship, nine 18-inch monsters, were sent out to face the Americans. Even though the Japanese had painfully taught the British that battleships facing hostile air and submarine cover don't last long at the start of their war, they repeated exactly that mistake. Towards the end of the conflict, in April 1945, the *Yamato* tried to intervene in the invasion of Okinawa, sent on a one-way mission without enough fuel to return. She didn't even get there. Think how many submarines the steel in those huge ships could have made.

34 The sunken guns fight back

THE 29,000-ton battleship *USS Arizona* is perhaps the most famous of the victims on 'Battleship Row' that terrible day at Pearl Harbor, lined up like sitting ducks for the Japanese surprise attack. Even while her men started to fight back, she blew up spectacularly when her magazine was hit by a bomb. She sank in shallow waters and unlike many of the other damaged ships, was never raised. Her twisted superstructure was scrapped during the war, and afterwards she became Hawaii's Pearl Harbor Memorial, with a visitor centre perched above the eerily visible hull which has been visited by millions of people.

But her huge submerged guns did fight back. Divers worked tirelessly to release them. The guns from Turret 2, which could lob their 14 inch diameter shells more than 10 miles, were installed on the *USS Nevada* and rained hell upon the heads of the Japanese forces dug into the islands of Okinawa and Iwo Jima, helping force their surrender. The surrender of the islands, that is – death was the outcome for most of the fanatical defenders. The other guns were installed as coastal defences in Hawaii. The huge weapons were far too valuable to waste.

Her fellow battleship, *USS Missouri,* a much more modern design, and in fact still being built at the time of the 1941 attack, and much larger at 45,000 tons, was moved to Pearl Harbor and moored as a museum ship some distance respectfully astern of the *Arizona* in 1999. She – nicknamed 'Mighty Mo' - earned a place in history as the ship on the deck of which the Japanese offered their unconditional surrender on September 2, 1945, with officers from all the Allied nations on deck.

The two battleships – one sunken, one proudly having fought in active service right up to the 1991 Gulf War – thus represent the two ends of the Second World War for America. A shocking loss, and ultimate victory. Two gigantic bookends.

Ghostly: The USS Arizona, still lying at Pearl Harbor, and today's memorial

35 The other 'Pearl Harbors'

THAT Pearl Harbor wasn't as unique as the rest of the world thinks is well known to most Australians. The massive raid on Darwin in the Northern Territories, on Tuesday, February 10, 1942, was even more one-sided than Pearl, and bigger in terms of tonnage of bombs.

The Japanese were to invade Timor the next day, and wanted to prevent any Allied interference from the south. They sent 242 aircraft to attack a weakly defended, ill-prepared town that would have had trouble fighting off a dozen planes, using four aircraft carriers that had attacked Pearl Harbor two months before. Casualties were heavy on the Australian side with 236 killed, 300–400 wounded, 30 aircraft destroyed, 11 vessels sunk, three grounded and 25 ships damaged. A recent movie depicting Japanese fighting on the ground was nonsense – they did not land. They didn't need to.

In fact about a third *more* bombs were dropped on Darwin that day than on Pearl Harbor. Casualties were lighter only because there were not any capital ships carrying thousands of men, so they were not being turned over and sunk. It wasn't a day of glory for Australia by any means – while there was some heroism, there was a lot more incompetence, disorganisation, looting and even, according to some sources, desertion (or wisely fleeing the scene, under confusing and ambiguous orders – it isn't clear).

An attack on Colombo, the port and capital of the British colony of Ceylon (now Sri Lanka), was potentially more disastrous for the Allied cause, and like Pearl Harbor, was conducted on a Sunday. In fact it was Easter Sunday, April 5, 1942, two months on from Darwin. British morale in Ceylon was poor, after the shattering loss on Singapore and two battleships near Malaya. Troops were jumpy – an Australian unit sounded the alarm that Japanese amphibious vessels were landing one day and it turned out to be large sea turtles. Defences were yet again lacking, despite this being the base for the British Eastern Fleet, pushed back from Singapore – a force that Japanese wanted that day to remove from Asian waters for ever.

But the British at least knew that the Japanese were coming. A flying boat had spotted the fleet the day before and got off a radio warning before being shot down. Even so, astonishingly, as at Darwin no radar was working (it was under routine maintenance). Many civilians and some servicemen were in church for Easter services.

The Ceylon *Daily News* on Monday, April 6, 1942 reported: 'Colombo and the suburbs were attacked yesterday at 8 o'clock in the morning by 75 enemy aircraft which came in waves from the sea. Twenty-five of the raiders were shot down, while 25 more were damaged. Dive-bombing and low-flying machine-gun attacks were made in the Harbour and Ratmalana areas. A medical establishment in the suburbs was also bombed.' That last place was, in fact, the city's lunatic asylum.

How serious this moment was for the British and Allies was revealed by Churchill in a dinner conversation with high-ranking

guests at the British Embassy in Washington, after the war. He said:

'The most dangerous moment of the War, and the one which caused me the greatest alarm, was when the Japanese Fleet was heading for Ceylon and the naval base there. The capture of Ceylon, the consequent control of the Indian Ocean, and the possibility at the same time of a German conquest of Egypt would have closed the ring and the future would have been black.'

But the fleet had been withdrawn to the Maldives, leaving only three ships and these were mostly under repair. There were more

deadly attacks on British ships around Ceylon over the next few days, sinking several, and a similar air assault on the port of Trincomalee, but most of the British Eastern Fleet escaped to fight another day. The survival of that fleet made a sea-borne invasion of Ceylon, and then India, impossible. Ironically, one of the ships caught at sea and sunk by the Japanese was *HMS Hermes*, the first aircraft carrier mentioned in item 6 and proudly shown to the Japanese. On that previous page, she is shown at her best. Here she is shown actually sinking, after the Japanese repaid the lessons she'd once taught; 307 of her men died.

The ship's name was reused for a different carrier – Britons will remember – that had an illustrious career later in the 20th century, including the Falklands War. But Churchill was right. Colombo *was* crucial. The resulting land assault on India through Burma would be beaten back by British Commonwealth forces in an exhausting and savage jungle campaign, showing the Japanese were not invincible after all. As at Pearl, and indeed Darwin, the Japanese would come to bitterly regret the fact that they had failed to make their knock-out blow that Easter Day at Colombo.

36 The ships that are not here

IN between the two battleships were hundreds - probably thousands - of other ships that went down in that terrible war. American, Japanese, British, Dutch, Australian - and others - many entombing their crews. Aircraft carriers - including the Japanese ones that launched the original sneak attack. Battleships - they are not just any warship, one has to explain nowadays, but the biggest surface fighting ships yet made, which on that day December 7, 1941, became as much the problem as the solution for naval power. The Japanese had learned well from their then British allies in the 1920s how to build and operate aircraft carriers, and now realised that 'flattops'- and submarines - represented the future of naval warfare. A lesson the Americans were learning the hard way that December day, and the British were to learn bitterly a few days later off Malaya. Famously, and luckily, the U.S. aircraft carriers were not at Pearl that day, and the subs were mostly unharmed too.

Ships that went down between these two titanic bookends included countless merchantmen – increasingly part of the effort to strangle and starve the Japanese economy. But among these were the 'hell ships' carrying enslaved Allied prisoners-of-war in appalling conditions, locked below decks and unable to escape when sunk.

One of these missing ships – the *Indianapolis,* pictured above, which had carried the atom bomb to within flying range of Japan, was torpedoed on her return on July 30, 1945 in shark-infested waters. That ship helped nail down the lid on the coffin of Japan's war-mongering dreams. But more horror, on a scale never seen before, was visited upon Hiroshima and Nagasaki, then yet more for the American crew members of that sunken heavy cruiser, unable to be quickly rescued because of radio silence rules. Of the 1,195 crew, only 316 survived the ordeal of sinking, starvation, thirst, exposure and shark attacks. It was the U.S. Navy's worst ever loss of life at sea from a single ship sinking.

All this unimaginable suffering and courage started right here in Pearl Harbor, and a few minutes earlier in Malaya for Britain. That it ended in victory is why we – Brits, Japanese, Americans and many others – could grow up in freedom to make what we did of our lives.

37 The rising death toll and the 'black tears'

OF THE about 1,000 men entombed in *Arizona* - it really wasn't sensible trying to piece together their remains in a ship where the magazine blew and twisted and pulverised enormously heavy metal armour, and then burned as hot as a crematorium for two days - the total is not fixed. It keeps increasing. Why? Because the surviving crew members have in recent decades been dying of old age and so far more than 40 have asked to rejoin their ship after death.

As a Navy woman told me when I visited: 'It's hard to explain what you feel for your ship. It's always a she. I've served in aircraft carriers – it's a belonging that lasts. These veterans want to rejoin their brothers. Not just Navy brothers, but real brothers often. There were many pairs of brothers aboard that day.'

The *Arizona*, you notice if you go on a calm day, continues even after 80 years to leak small amounts of oil, with an iridescence on the surface giving those rainbow colours when the sun strikes them. Or as a sentimentalist put it, 'She weeps black tears. She will only stop when the last man returns.' Yes, it's a form of pollution. But it means so much more.

38 A baby remains in the wreck

AMONG the remains still on the wreck of the *USS Utah* are the remains of a baby girl. Nancy Lynne Wagner was just two days old when she died, and her grief-stricken father Albert Wagner took her ashes aboard intending to scatter them at sea. It never happened. She is in the Navy for ever now, her remains – as her twin sister put it after the war – eternally guarded by her shipmates who died that day.

39 Operation Vengeance: Get Yamamoto!

THE deliberate targeting of another country's military or political leader is rare, maybe because politicians and generals who would make such a decision could be the next target. A recent famous case was the American vow to nail Osama Bin Laden, architect of the 9/11 attacks on New York, killed in 2011, after years of hunting him.

The case echoed the U.S. determination to kill Admiral Isoroku Yamamoto of the Imperial Japanese Navy, mastermind of the 1941 attack at Pearl Harbor. Just as with Bin Laden, the operation was brilliantly executed, highly secret and ruthlessly calculated.

Oddly enough, Yamamoto (pictured here) had not wanted to attack the United States, and thought it would end in trouble. He didn't hate the Americans: he'd studied at Harvard and worked in

Washington as a naval attaché, travelling throughout the States. He knew the country's vast resources, both natural, industrial and indeed human, would make the USA difficult to out-fight in the long run.

Forced to accept war with America, however, he planned a brilliant knock-out blow, or at least a preventative strike, enabling Japan to seize the oil and rubber producing colonies of British Malaya and the Dutch East Indies. Even so, he thought the attack on Pearl would rebound on Japan disastrously within two to three years – in which he was absolutely right.

Yamamoto was an interestingly independent thinker. He had spoken out bravely against Japan's invasion of Manchuria in 1931 and the following war with China. He was also against the tripartite pact with Nazi Germany and Fascist Italy, which he thought would drag Japan into disaster. Bravely because he received many death threats from the military hard-liners and had to have an armed guard to protect him, eventually being sent back to sea to save him.

He wrote about this threat to him, and it is interesting to quote it as a possible glimpse into the mindset of the man:

To die for Emperor and Nation is the highest hope of a military man. After a brave hard fight the blossoms are scattered on the fighting field. But if a person wants to take a life instead, still the fighting man will go to eternity for Emperor and country. One man's life or death is a matter of no importance. All that matters is the Empire ... They may destroy my body, yet they will not take away my will.

But beware the tendency to lionise foreign military leaders – Rommel, for example. What where they fighting *for*?

This quotation might seem in a novel about the Samurai ethos to be rather poetic and beautiful but is it in fact sane? This was about real people dying by the thousands. To die a possibly horrible death for a cruel regime that was torturing thousands of prisoners, bombing, raping and murdering civilians, seizing and enslaving whole countries for naked imperialism? Was it beautiful?

To put it another way, we in the West had learned horribly in World War I that 'dulce et decorum est pro patria mori' – the Latin tag meaning it is sweet and fitting to die for one's country – might not seem 100 per cent true when dying in a cold Somme shellhole with terrible wounds in a war started for no clear purpose. The Japanese had not yet tried living in peace, freedom and democracy, but when they did, after the war, such attitudes as Yamamoto expressed were respected, but seen more as something from history than a code to live by. If you compare his quotation to something from the jihadists wanting to die for their cause today, also believing they are going to some paradise, and well …. it isn't about blossoms and never was.

But he was a charismatic, intelligent man, and while he may have meant what he wrote, it might have been the kind of thing you put down in calligraphy – which was a hobby of his – and may not in practice follow quite so blindly. His record suggests he was more sceptical and thoughtful.

The career naval officer, son of a samurai, a brilliant tactician and commander, he was protected against dismissal by his deep popularity with the men of the IJN, which reached adulation after the

Pearl Harbor attack succeeded, and his close links to the Imperial family. Thus his loss would be a massive blow to Japanese morale. The chance came in 1943.

By then, Japan's new conquest were beginning to be eaten away – defeat at Guadalcanal made Yamamoto decide on a morale-boosting inspection tour of the outlying islands. Local commanders were sent his itinerary in code – a code the Americans had cracked. It revealed he and his staff would be in two bombers landing in the Solomon Islands, escorted by a few fighters, on the morning of April 18, 1943. The bombers, officially code-named 'Bettys' by the Americans, were nicknamed by U.S. pilots the 'Flying Cigarette Lighters' because they were easy to set ablaze.

Roosevelt – who had personally ordered 'bomb Tokio' in the Doolittle raids the previous year – now ordered 'get Yamamoto'.

Operation Vengeance called for an interception from Guadalcanal. Using a roundabout route to avoid alerting the enemy, this would be 1,000 miles, the longest fighter interception in history. The only aircraft which could hope to do this was the twin-engined P-38 Lightning, if fitted with extra drop tanks.

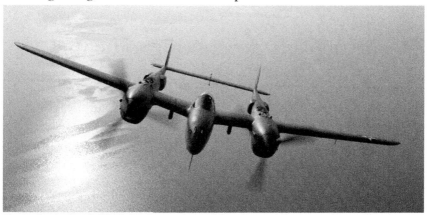

Fast, sleek, the P-38 Lightning, selected for the task to assassinate Yamamoto

The interception worked brilliantly, arriving to the minute after the long legs of the journey flying at just 50ft over the waves to keep their passage secret. Both the 'Betty' bombers were shot down and Yamamoto was killed.

Japan was stunned. His ashes were returned in a battleship for a state funeral amidst massive public mourning. In America, many felt Pearl Harbor had been avenged.

40 The forgotten British carriers

THE Pacific war after Pearl Harbor is rightly portrayed as the Americans v the Japanese. But just as the U.S. came to the free world's help in liberating Europe, so British and indeed Australian ships came to aid the U.S. Navy in the Pacific, and this forgotten effort involved Royal Navy aircraft carriers – with odd consequences.

The Japanese had failed to sink the U.S. aircraft carriers at Pearl Harbor, but later in the war desperately tried to rectify that crucial omission by famously employing kamikaze suicide pilots who could put an American aircraft carrier out of action for months, or sink it. But British carriers had meanwhile arrived in the Pacific with armoured decks.

'It was amazing,' said one U.S. observer quoted by a British newspaperman. 'The Jap planes came in and kerpow! they hit the carrier. It would have put us into Pearl for a month. The Limeys just brushed off the wreckage and got on with flying planes. I'd have given anything to see the last look on that Jap's face.' This may be an exaggeration of how light the damage was, but the carriers were back in action within an hour.

41 The unlikely deception: Some tug!

BRITISH sailors say that for the passage through the Panama Canal of one such carrier, the *Victorious* was listed at *USS Robin*, a small tug. If so, the disguise can't have fooled any Japanese spies lurking around Panama for very long. This may be just naval legend, as may be their statement that on the way back from service with the American fleet, *Victorious* stopped off in September, 1943, to drop off her ice cream-making machines and Coca-Cola dispensers – there were probably more serious adjustments to make for changing back to the Atlantic war! What is true is that in the Pacific, the U.S. Admiral realised how good the RN ship's fighter direction system was, and sent *Victorious* fighter aircraft only, better suited to her catapults anyway, leaving its American companion, the *USS Saratoga,* to run the bombers.

42 The U.S. cruiser sunk by the British

THE 10,650-ton light cruiser *USS Phoenix* survived the 1941 surprise Japanese attack on Pearl Harbor by weighing anchor and escaping, only to be sunk by the British ... 41 years later. In 1982, by then renamed the *General Belgrano* and part of the Argentine forces trying to seize the Falklands, the *Belgrano* with her 15 six-inch long-range guns and Sea Cat anti-aircraft missiles was judged a threat to the task force carrying thousands of men and their equipment from Britain to retake the islands and so was sunk by submarine.

The USS Phoenix escapes the Pearl Harbor attack, steaming past the burning West Virginia and Arizona. In the long run, a different enemy awaited

43 The last hurrah of the heavy guns

THE *Pheonix* - the *Belgrano* to be - had already secured a place in naval history, when she took part on October 25, 1944 in the last major naval battle involving capital ships slogging it out with heavy gunfire. The *Phoenix*, the *USS Boise* and the Australian cruiser *Shropshire* fired 1,181 rounds from their main batteries in 17 minutes to help pulverise the Japanese fleet in the Battle of Surigao Strait, part of three-day Battle of Leyte Gulf. This was how admirals imagined naval war to be at the start of the conflict – but more and more the opposing vessels were invisible over the horizon, fighting with air fleets, or under water in deadly submarine attacks.

In fact at this epoch-ending night battle the Americans had no fewer than six battleships waiting for the Japanese, who were trying to sneak through a strait to attack U.S. forces.

These were the *West Virginia, Maryland, Mississippi, Tennessee, Pennsylvania and California*. All of these except *Mississippi* had been sunk or damaged at the Pearl Harbor attack, but had been raised, salvaged and repaired by Herculean efforts.

This showed that even the ships which the Japanese hit – and they missed the absolutely crucial submarines and aircraft carriers, remember – were mostly *not* knocked out of the war as they had hoped.

Awesome: The broadside of a battleship. This is a picture taken at a later date

At this battle the Japanese thus faced a staggering amount of fire-power, radar controlled at night, plus having to run the gauntlet of seemingly endless U.S. torpedo boats and destroyers in the narrows. The Japanese fired blindly in all directions and achieved little except to show themselves more clearly as targets.

Their losses in what is often said to be the largest naval battle in history were simply appalling: 12,500 dead, 1 fleet carrier, 3 light carriers, 3 battleships, 10 cruisers, 11 destroyers, and about 300 aircraft. For the Japanese, this was far worse than Pearl Harbor for the U.S. – and they had simply no way of replacing the losses.

It seem suicidal for the Japanese to throw their fleet into the battle like this, although they could not have known how mighty the forces were ranged against them and clearly thought they might catch the Americans unawares. Interestingly, one of their admirals said under later interrogation that it was worth the gamble. If they lost the Philippines, the fleet would have been useless anyway:

'Should we lose in the Philippines operations, even though the fleet should be left, the shipping lane to the south would be completely cut off so that the fleet, if it should come back to Japanese waters, could not obtain its fuel supply. If it should remain in southern waters, it could not receive supplies of ammunition and arms. There would be no sense in saving the fleet at the expense of the loss of the Philippines.'

So the *Phoenix,* which had earlier steamed out of Pearl Harbor during that attack, played her part in this historic night. Then, as the *General Belgrano,* she made another entry in naval history: the first ship in history to be sunk by a nuclear-powered submarine, *HMS Conqueror,* using two conventional torpedoes, ironically finishing the job Japanese aviators were trying so hard to do 41 years earlier.

The General Belgrano, sinking in 1982, having escaped Pearl Harbor in 1941

44 The very odd relics in Britain

EVEN that had a macabre sequel which has survived into the 21st century. The periscopes from *Conqueror* were salvaged when the boat was scrapped, and they are part of the submarine museum at Gosport, Hampshire. A spokesman was quoted as saying 'Visitors are made aware that they're from the *Conqueror* but not many realise the implications. We'd get a lot more interest if we stuck a big note on them saying: "These periscopes were used to dispatch 300 Argentinians", but it might be a bit gruesome.'

The other major Argentine ship at the time of the Falklands War – an aircraft carrier called the *ARA Veinticinco de Mayo* – was not originally American. But she was once *HMS Venerable*, one of the four World War II British carriers that had joined the American war in the Pacific, and perhaps wisely stayed in port until the 1982 fighting was over, and was later scrapped, except for one part still functioning – the bell of St Mary's church in Ash Vale, near Aldershot, Hampshire, can be seen, on close examination, to be inscribed 'HMS Venerable 1944'.

The incredible attack on Pearl Harbor as told from both the American and Japanese sides.

From 20th Century-Fox. The most spectacular film ever made.

45 Genda's second go around

COMMANDER Genda was paid twice for helping plan the attack on Pearl Harbor - once by the Japanese and once by America, in the form of Twentieth-Century Fox, who wanted his advice on a re-enactment of Pearl Harbor for the blockbuster film *Tora! Tora! Tora!*.

46 The film fakes

THE *Tora! Tora! Tora!* film-makers painstakingly built a brilliant replica of one of the ships sunk in the attack at a cost of £600,000 .... then bombed and sunk it all over again. The shots of 'Japanese' aircraft taking off from a carrier in the middle of the vast Pacific were in fact American trainer aircraft taking off from a disguised American carrier off San Diego. Because the fake planes could not land on the carrier again, so they to land ashore and the carrier had to go and fetch them for the next scene.

47 The rather real crash scenes…

Those may have been fake but some of the footage was worryingly real. The scene where a Flying Fortress crash-lands *was* real – it had faulty undercarriage and one wheel would not go down. And the scene where men run for their lives as a Japanese plane crashes into a line of parked planes was real too. It was supposed to crash into the other end. So they really *were* running for their lives. The 2001 movie, *Pearl Harbor*, cost much more but was a relative flop.

48 The last victims...

IN June 1991 the Pearl Harbor saga claimed two more American lives. Two pilots flying a partial re-enactment at a Florida air show clipped wings and crashed.

49 The traitor who escaped Scot-free

One of the worst things about Britain in the 20th century was the stream of posh, deluded, often Left-wing spies who betrayed their country and its allies with terrible consequences and often escaped scot-free when they would have been hanged as the despicable the traitors they undoubtedly were, had they been working-class.

William Forbes-Sempill, the 19th Lord Sempill, was certainly posh: castle in Scotland (Craigievar Castle, pictured left, now run by the National Trust), educated at Eton, social links to the Royal

Family. He certainly escaped the noose that any fair judgment by the standards of the day would have put around his neck. He certainly did massive damage to Britain and the USA, helping causing untold suffering to millions by his equipping the enemy – as it turned out – with the latest technology. He was certainly deluded. But he wasn't a Lefty, and although in fact a fascist sympathiser (then fairly fashionable in the upper classes, who had little idea what it would lead to) wasn't really committed to any ideology. So what drove him to do it? He seems to have been a truculent, malevolent, rebellious, arrogant mischief-maker who just 'went native' – meaning he joined the cause of the people where he was sent to represent his country. The Japanese.

Born in 1893, son of a Scots laird, Forbes-Sempill joined the

Royal Flying Corps in World War I, then moved into the RAF when that was formed, then into naval aviation, with a spot of test-pilot work too. He even, later, gained a few aviation records – one for the first non-stop flight from Croydon aerodrome to Berlin in 1936. It was welcomed as a step forward in civil aviation, (although within five years thousands of fliers would be making non-stop runs between Britain and Germany, for rather different purposes).

So far, so respectable a biography.

And when, back in 1920, he led a British civilian mission of former naval airmen to Japan, this was respectable too. They had been our useful World War I ally, and still were, and the British Government saw a chance of lucrative arms contracts – to help Japan develop aircraft carriers (a very new concept – Britain was at the time building the world's first purpose-built, rather than adapted, carrier).

Captain Sempill is pictured showing a Gloster Sparrowhawk to Admiral Togo Heihachiro in 1921.

The Japanese had just bought three Supermarine flying boats, and the Air Ministry thought they might buy lots more British equipment. (In fact, as with the Soviet Union after World II and China in recent years, this could have been a mistake. They wanted to find out all about the latest technology, by fair means or foul, and then make their version better, which they certainly did.)

With the ending of the Anglo-Japanese Alliance in 1921, Sempill should have ended such close contact on military matters and not had any discussions about naval aviation, technology and tactics. But on his return to Britain in 1923, Sempill kept in contact with the Foreign Ministry in Tokio through the Japanese Embassy in London. He was a respected figure in Japan, and this flattery clearly got to him – even the Prime Minister, Kato Tomosaburo, wrote him a personal letter, thanking him for his work with the Imperial Japanese Navy, which he described as 'almost epoch-making'. It certainly would be at Pearl Harbor, Singapore and Hong Kong within 20 years.

As well as a tale of treachery, this is a story of official complacency, snobbery and bungling. Why? Because although it was clearly suspected, and eventually known, by the British authorities that he was a spy from 1922, he carried on doing serious damage and being given access to more and more sensitive documents for 20 years, even into the war he helped cause. All because he was posh and imperious.

The Directorate of Military Intelligence had kept Sempill's communications with the Japanese naval attaché (and spy) in London, Captain Teijirō Toyoda, under surveillance from 1922. They could see Sempill was passing classified information to the Japanese, which Toyoda's messages back to Tokio indicated had been paid for. MI5 had also tapped Sempill's telephone, and knew that his servant was a Japanese naval rating.

In 1925 Japanese intelligence asked Sempill to obtain top secret technical data about the prototype of the Blackburn Iris seaplane (right). Sempill accompanied a delegation of foreign air officials to the Blackburn Aircraft factory at Brough, near Hull. The Japanese had been monitored asking Sempill particular questions about the aircraft being developed. Sempill later asked *exactly the same questions*, in his semi-official capacity, about the still-secret Blackburn Iris.

On the train to Brough, Sempill had openly talked about details of the Iris with the foreign air officials. This was witnessed by an Air Ministry civil servant, who reported it. Confronted with this information, Sempill admitted that he had broken the Official Secrets Act.

Sempill was called into the Foreign Office for questioning. The aim was to assess his loyalty to Britain, and to Japan, and to find out what he had leaked to the Japanese. But the interview had to take place without the investigating officer revealing that the British had broken Japanese codes and were monitoring the Japanese communications systems, so he was unable to confront Sempill with cast-iron proof of his betrayal.

A meeting was called to discuss the case in Whitehall, chaired by Foreign Secretary Austen Chamberlain. It was argued not to put Sempill on trial for two reason. One, Sempill's father was *aide-de-camp* to the King, and it would cause serious embarrassment to the Crown and the Government. Two, it would compromise security by letting the Japanese government know their codes had been broken.

In the 1930s, Sempill started working as a consultant in Europe for Japan's Mitsubishi Heavy Industries, and also became chairman and then president of the Royal Aeronautical Society, allowing him to advise several other countries, including Australia, on how to organise their naval air services… while all the time secretly spying for the country that would act to destroy them within ten years. During this time, while in a car in the USA racing to meet the German Zeppelin, he suffered a serious crash in which he was injured – not seriously enough, some might think – although his driver died. On the death of his father, not long afterwards, he became Lord Sempill and Baronet of Craigievar, taking his seat in the House of Lords as a Tory peer.

He became sympathetic to the militarist Right-wing regimes then emerging, and joined anti-Semitic and pro-Nazi groups. Despite all this, on the outbreak of war in September, 1939, Lord Sempill was given a position in the Department of Air Materiel, part of the Admiralty, which meant he could see sensitive and secret information about the latest British aircraft. Why? Presumably because he was right in the Establishment. This was also the era where Japanese aviation – fighter aircraft, bombers, aircraft carriers, etc –was secretly leaping ahead of the West's. How much of this was with Sempill's help we will never know, but if he sped up Japanese aviation development by about five years, this seemed to be the advantage when their Zeroes and bombers easily outclassed British and American planes at the start of the war.

In early 1941, Sempill intervened when a Japanese businessman was arrested and taken to a London police station on charges of spying. Sempill used his position to get the man released.

In mid-1941, MI5 intercepted messages between London and Tokio indicating that Sempill was being paid for information and was useful to them. It was suspected he was passing on secrets. Again it was recommended that he be arrested and charged, but again the Attorney General advised against prosecution. Why? Probably because he was posh, powerful and the 'friend of a friend' who was the 'right sort of chap'. On September 5, 1941, Sempill was called into a meeting with the Fifth Sea Lord for 'a strict private warning'.

Sempill was also passing on detailed information about the British government. When British PM Winston Churchill famously met U.S. President Frankin Roosevelt on *HMS Prince of Wales* in Newfoundland to discuss the Japanese threat (only months before Pearl Harbor, and on a ship that would be sunk shortly afterwards by the Japanese with aircraft improved with Sempill's help), soon afterwards the Japanese Embassy was sending transcripts of what was discussed back to Tokio. A deeply worried Churchill saw this and said the information was 'pretty accurate'. Three months later, more government political secrets were being sent to Tokio, and Churchill decided it must be Sempill. Was he arrested and shot?

No, in October 1941 – just two months before this enemy would attack us – Churchill simply wrote: 'Clear him out while time remains.' The next week Sempill was told by his superiors that he must either resign or be sacked.

After Sempill made an official protest, Churchill backtracked. The PM feebly told the Admiralty: 'I had not contemplated Lord Sempill being required to resign his commission, but only to be employed elsewhere in the Admiralty.' It was suggested somewhere in the North of Scotland, without much access to secrets, and monitored by MI5 would be a good idea.

Then Japan attacked in December 1941 – and against British colonies slightly before Pearl Harbor, as it happened. A few days later, Sempill's office was searched. Secret documents were found that should not have been there. Two days later Sempill was found to be telephoning the Japanese.

Was he shot or hanged? We were, after all, now at war with the very people he was helping! No. He was asked to retire from public life, which he did with bad grace. He went on to live a comfortable post-war life, (not a privilege enjoyed by those tortured and beheaded by his friends, the Japanese invaders), becoming president of the British Gliding Association and the Institute of Advanced Motorists. He died in 1965, not a moment too soon, his reputation still intact as a responsible member of the Establishment. His title was still the medal-wearing (Japanese as well as British) The Right Honourable The Lord Sempill. *Honourable?* It's absolutely sickening.

A powerful comparison can be made with Alan Turing (pictured), the British mathematics genius who was the key brains behind the Bletchley Park team who famously broke Germany's fantastically complex Enigma code. Turing was a homosexual, then of course illegal, and was prosecuted for this after the war and encouraged to undergo 'chemical castration' to end any such urges, as an alternative to prison. He seems to have killed himself in 1954, shortly after this treatment, in some torment.

A lonely, miserable death – he should have rightly been given a knighthood for shortening the war by perhaps two years and saving millions of lives – while the traitor Sempill carried in his life of privilege. Turing was the 'right honourable' one of the two. Even allowing for the fact that fashion has swung towards people like Turing and away from people like Sempill (rightly, in my view), the injustice was huge. If the Germans had had two years more of war, would they have finished developing the atomic bomb? They already had the unstoppable V2 missiles that could reach London by 1945. This could be what Turing saved us from.

Today Turing is remembered in books, films, in maths departments of universities around the world and in plaques at his birthplace in Maida Vale, London, and his place of death in Wilmslow, Cheshire (pictured).

Sempill's disgraceful story, however, was and is glossed over. It was the worst that the age of deference to one's supposed betters produced. Churchill comes out of the account as craven and weak. As the barbarically cruel Japanese raped, bayonetted and tortured their way through the patients

ALAN TURING
1912 - 1954
Founder of computer science
and cryptographer, whose work
was key to breaking the
wartime Enigma codes,
lived and died here.

and nurses in the hospitals in Singapore and Hong Kong, I don't suppose it would have been any comfort to the dying victims if they had known at least the enemy's posh friend in Britain had been protected by the Establishment. Scotland has so many military heroes it should be deeply proud of – and I write as grandson of a Scots soldier – but this was one man of whom it should be ashamed.

50 How Elvis Presley got involved

ELVIS PRESLEY, who would have been a six-year-old boy when the Pearl Harbor attack took place, was instrumental in getting the *USS Arizona* memorial you see today built. He got behind the appeal for funds, staged a benefit concert on March 25, 1961 and raised the then huge sum of $64,000.

(This event should not be confused with the concert better known to Elvis fans called *Aloha from Hawaii Via Satellite* staged 12 years later. It was billed as the first live concert sent by satellite around the world – which it wasn't – and the reason for choosing

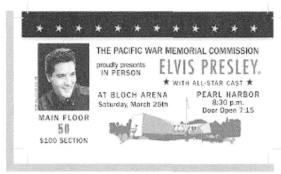

Hawaii was not known to fans at the time. Elvis's manager 'Colonel' Tom Parker was secretly an illegal immigrant and thus refused all overseas tours – Elvis never appeared in Britain, for example – fearing deportation back to the Netherlands if he tried to re-enter the United States. Parker, real name Andreas Cornelis van Kuijk, wanted somewhere exotic for the broadcast and thus picked Hawaii, exciting – but still safely in the USA.)

51 The ignorance of history

EVEN then British Prime Minister Tony Blair seems to have misunderstood the significance of Pearl Harbor. Speaking on September 20, 2001 in New York after the service for the victims of the September 11 tragedy, he said: 'My father's generation knew what it was like. They went through the Blitz. They knew what it was like to suffer the tragedy of attack. The Americans stood side by side with us then.' No they didn't! The Blitz was largely over before Pearl Harbor forced America into the war. Even then, most people believe the U.S. declared war on Germany. It didn't. It was the other way round, because Italy and Germany were bound by a pact with Japan to support them.

It fact the U.S. didn't even declare war on Japan first – that was Britain, having suffered the first attack in Japan's campaign (which is where we came in, in item 1). But in the end, it was what mattered – the Americans were by our side again.

All in all, it's a still astonishing, compelling story, better understood, I hope, with these 50 little-known but fascinating pieces of the jigsaw. If we have less ignorance of history than some of our leaders they might not lead us into repeating past errors.

At least Churchill at the time understood what Pearl Harbor meant. He wrote of that evening:

I went to bed and slept the sleep of the saved and the thankful.

What followed: The fight across the Pacific is epitomised by this iconic photo at Iwo Jima. In fact this was restaged for the camera after the real moment

A less familiar picture: An M4 Sherman tank that never made it to the beach still stands today in the sea, seemingly still ready to fight. (Asahi Shimbun)

BONUS CHAPTERS: UNLIKELY WARS

THE GREAT EMU WAR: This is back in the 1930s, when the military might of the Australian state – in the form of Major G.P.W. Meredith of the Seventh Heavy Battery of the Royal Australian Artillery – took on an apparently easy-to-defeat enemy: the emu, an ostrich-like bird.

Given that the emu cannot fly, is generally unarmed and untrained, and is an easy target at six foot tall, and that the soldiers were armed with Lewis guns and 10,000 rounds of ammunition, it should have been a walk-over. In fact the emu was the clear victor.

I say *the* emu, but there were lots of them – about 20,000 – and to be (briefly) fair to the authorities for a moment, the emus made a mass attack on farms in Western Australia. The birds ravaged the crops and tore holes in the fencing so whole regiments of rabbits could join in on their side. The farmers – mostly veterans of the First World War who had been encouraged to settle there, just in time for the Great Depression to slash prices for their crops – were desperate and pleaded for drastic government action.

In October 1932, the military expedition arrived in the Campion district. Hostilities were delayed by heavy rain, which had the effect of breaking up the emu army into small detachments. On November 2, the campaign started with farmers attempting to herd the emus towards the waiting guns. However stupid emus may be, they weren't having any of this (unlike, one must reluctantly say, the soldiers in the recently finished war, who were slaughtered). The emu ranks broke up into small groups running off in all directions. The Lewis guns opened fire, but the range was too great and hardly a bird was hit.

Australian troops with a Lewis gun (on a later occasion)

Another skirmish later in the day resulted in only a few dozen emu fatalities.

On November 4, Meredith tried to be more cunning. He set an ambush at a local dam with one of the Lewis guns. A force of 1,000 emus was seen approaching, and the gunner held his fire until he could see the beady eyes of the critters. He opened fire, but soon the gun jammed and only 12 of 'the enemy' were accounted for.

In the following days, Meredith moved his forces south towards the apparent emu HQ, or rather where they seemed more docile. He made the mistake of mounting one of the guns on a truck. This bumped and lurched over the rough ground so it could not keep up

with the emus or aim accurately. The bullets flew everywhere – endangering nearby farmers – but hit very few emus.

By November 8, emu forces (a humorous mock-up picture is shown of one emu participant, left) were outflanking the military in an embarrassing way. Local ornithologist Dominic Serventy commented:

The machine-gunners' dreams of point blank fire into serried masses of Emus were soon dissipated. The Emu command had evidently ordered guerrilla tactics, and its unwieldy army soon split up into innumerable small units that made use of the military equipment uneconomic. A crestfallen field force therefore withdrew from the combat area after about a month.

Major Meredith was forced to explain to the Defence Minister his force's humiliation, and he paid this unlikely tribute to the emu 'enemy', who carried on even after being hit several times:

If we had a military division with the bullet-carrying capacity of these birds it would face any army in the world... They can face machine guns with the invulnerability of tanks. They are like Zulus whom even dum-dum bullets could not stop.

The unimpressed and obstinate Minister of Defence, Sir George Pearce, seemed to stick his head in the sand like an, erm, ostrich. He ordered a second campaign which started in late November and lasted into December. Instead of tens of thousands of emus being killed as hoped, the numbers were about a 40 a day. Soon, all the ammo – which the farmers were forced to pay for – was expended, and the Army withdrew, leaving the emu ranks to be reformed. It was a national humiliation for the mighty Australian military – defeated by a bunch of overgrown chickens!

Emu War	
Part of The Great Depression	
Date	1932
Location	Campion, Western Australia
Result	Decisive Emu Victory
Belligerents	
Commonwealth of Australia	Emus
Commanders	
Major Meredith	none
Strength	
2 machine guns	20 000 birds
Casualties and losses	
10 000 rounds of ammo. Dignity.	12 birds+

How One internet page summed up the Emu War.
Note the caustic comment on losses!

PS: If you read anywhere of co-ordinated emus converging on London from all directions, don't panic! It happens every day. It's a railwayman's acronym for electric multiple units – commuter trains.

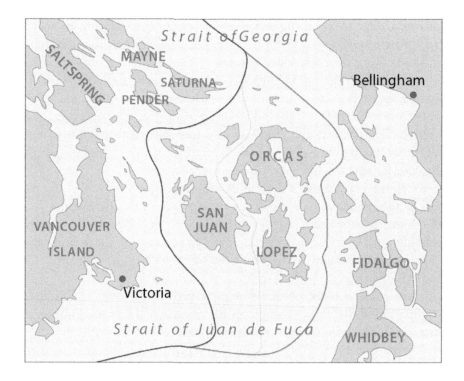

THE PIG WAR OF 1859: This war on the U.S./Canadian border involved hundreds of men from the United States and British forces, three warships, colonels and captains, a rear admiral, dozens of cannon, tons of ammunition and other stores, the Kaiser of Germany, top diplomats, international conferences around the world … and a pig. Only one shot was fired … at the pig. Only one casualty was recorded …the pig.

The trouble had started because of a treaty between the United States and Great Britain about where the boundary between Oregon and Columbia district (today part of Canada) would run. The treaty said the boundary would run along the 49th parallel 'to the middle of the channel which separates the continent from Vancouver Island and thence southerly through the middle of the said channel … to the Pacific Ocean.' Fine, except no one had taken a look.

There was no middle of the channel – it split in half around some islands, San Juan in particular (see map, above). Not too much of a problem until a chap called Lyman Cutlar, an American failed gold prospector, arrived on the island to claim the land as his farm and grow potatoes. On the morning on June 15, 1859, it all started to go wrong. Cutlar found a pig snaffling his potatoes – digging them up half-grown, no less – and took umbrage, took out his rifle, took aim and took a pot shot. He killed the pig.

It turned out the pig belonged to a local Irishman, Charles Griffin, who thought he was in a part of the British Empire, not the USA. This almost started a full-scale border war (the two countries has been belligerents several times in the previous century, the British famously having burned down the White House in Washington about 40 years earlier).

Both men appealed to their authorities for protection from the pig and potato debacle. In a ludicrous over-reaction, the Americans sent 66 men to stop the piggery jokery, and the British sent three warships. Cannon were shipped in to either end of the island, and flags raised. Would there soon be a crackling of gunfire? Or something rasher?

Fortunately a bit of common sense saved their bacon. The military occupation and stand-off went on for an insane 12 years. During all that time the two camps fraternised, celebrating national holidays with each other, the British laying out a formal garden next to their warship, and both sides consuming much alcohol and competing on sports days. Orders from London and Washington to take a sterner line were studiously ignored and not one more shot was fired. Local commanders expressed the view it would be ludicrous to spill blood over pork and potatoes.

In the end of the boundary question was referred to Kaiser Wilhelm I of Germany, who had never heard of the place, let along visited it. He set up a commission to investigate. It ran for a whole year in Geneva, Switzerland, and also never visited the place. It ruled in favour of the Americans, who were losing interest because of their Civil War (their local commander quit his post to go and fight against the government he had just been standing up for).

Today, the island is a tourist attraction. The pig that nearly started a full-scale war is forgotten. But every day, U.S. government employees raise a flag at the spot known as English Camp. A Union Jack.

THE WAR OF THE STRAY DOG: This war in 1925 started with a trivial cause, like the War of the Pig (above) and in this case the dog wasn't even killed. But the result was far from trivial, with at least 50 and possibly over 100 people – mostly civilians – killed in the one week before it was over. And it included an early and effective intervention of the League of Nations, the peace-keeping precursor of the United Nations set up after the First World War.

On October 25, 1925, a Greek soldier's dog strayed across the border with Bulgaria at a place called the Pass of Demirkapia, near the Bulgarian border town of Petrich. The soldier nipped across the border to grab the errant animal – at which point a Bulgarian sentry shot him (the Greek soldier, not the dog) dead.

Oddly enough, considering what happened later, the Bulgarians were quick to express regret, to say it was due to a misunderstanding, and to offer to set up a joint commission to investigate why the shooting happened.

The Greek government, under dictator Theodoros Pangalos, was having none of this. It issued a three-point ultimatum to Bulgaria:

1 . Punishment of those responsible.

2 An official apology by the Bulgarian state.

3. Two million French francs in compensation.

Failing to wait for this to take effect, it also sent its soldiers to attack and occupy the town of Petrich. This led to the deaths of 50 Bulgarians, mostly civilians. The accounts differ, however, with the Bulgars claiming 121 Greeks killed.

The League of Nations was involved very rapidly, and ordered a ceasefire by telegraph. It judged Greece's actions needlessly aggressive, and ordered:

1 An immediate ceasefire.

2 All Greeks troops to withdraw from Bulgaria.

3 Compensation of £45,000 to be paid by the Greeks, and

British, French and Italian observers to monitor this whole process. Both sides complied, but the Greeks were humiliated and complained that there were double standards here – when Italian aggression started the Corfu Incident only two years earlier, Italy (which launched a major attack on that island causing about 20 deaths and 30 injuries) was not punished but the League of Nations ordered Italy to be compensated by Greece. The Greeks felt there was one rule for the great powers – in that case the bullying Italy – and one for the minor countries.

But in the War of the Stray Dog, why did one passportless pet pooch cause such mayhem? Well, for something so minor to trigger a major explosion, the situation has to be loaded with tensions beforehand. The background to the War of the Stray Dog was a period of tension, border war, territorial dispute, guerrilla action and assassination between the neighbouring countries since the start of the 20th century. It is not known what eventually became of the stray dog – the picture, although appealing, is not of the particular animal, and the flag shown is that of Greece – but this short war left a legacy of local bitterness that took decades to dissipate.

THE WAR OF PORK AND BEANS: Was a similar U.S./Canadian barney to the 1859 Pig War (above), at the other end of their land border. This 'war' in the U.S. state of Maine (then a part of Massachusetts), was similar in that no one was killed by direct military action, although forces were called out to confront each other. But different in that the two sides somehow managed to lose 38 men through accidents and disease (the grave shown, below, was erected much later, and is of a man who was run over by one of his own U.S. Army wagons, and not in an Indian War but this one. The wagon may well have been carrying pork and beans – certainly that's what the Maine troops complained of eating all the way through the months of confrontation).

It took place in 1839-42, 20 years earlier than the Pig War, so the Americans' potential enemy was the British North America, rather than Canada, and the border was far from clear, which is what it was all about. It's also called the Aroostook War after a river valley involved, but either way, it had consequences for both countries.

The trouble was the 1783 Treaty of Paris which ended the American Revolutionary War failed to mark the boundary between British North America and the USA. In what is now northern Maine, then beginning to be settled by Americans, conflict arose with what they considered to be invading, stealing lumberjacks from New Brunswick in Canada.

The thing started with posses being sent out to confront each other, escalated with locals arming themselves by breaking into an armoury, an attempt by the British to arrest some of the leaders trying to form a township in the American side, the calling out of militias, and the building of forts, barracks and blockhouses. Regular Army regiments were also called to the confrontation.

It was complicated by the involvement of one black bear and potentially of French settlers – the bear joined in the Battle of Caribou on December 29, 1838. This was a skirmish between Maine and New Brunswick lumbermen in which the Americans accused the northerners of stealing timber. As armed parties confronted each other, a black bear attacked, causing shots to be fired at it and general firing to break out by men who assumed the other side fired first. Luckily, they all missed and went home. Except the bear.

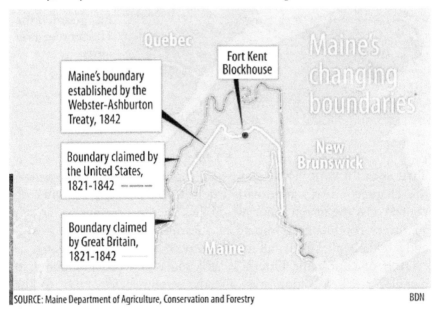

SOURCE: Maine Department of Agriculture, Conservation and Forestry   BDN

The French Canadians were Acadians – left over from failed French attempts to colonise Canada and Louisiana - who were nominally British Crown subjects but in fact claimed to be freemen and in a republic of their own. There were too small in number to make any difference, but their sympathies were with the Americans, not Queen Victoria.

In the end, two politicians, Webster and Ashburton, saw sense, but not until after King William I of the Netherlands had been called in to arbitrate – and been ignored – and maps had been produced by both sides and then hidden or faked, according to whom you believe.

With the Webster-Ashburton Treaty in 1842 fixing the current-day border, the British achieved what they wanted most – to keep military access to New Brunswick from Quebec and keep the Americans away from the seaway to the north. The Americans got most of the land they thought was theirs. Locals on both sides claimed that their respective governments let them down.

Left: Fort Kent, complete with gun slits, built during the Pork and Beans War, has guarded the U.S. border ever since

* * * * *

THE SOCCER WAR: This sounds like the most trivial of the wars in this chapter – as it started with a defeat on a soccer pitch after one country lost the match – but was in fact the most serious so far, with air forces conducting bombing raids, armour and artillery involved, and 3,000 people killed – all for no purpose or long-term effect.

And of course the bitterness and anger between Honduras and neighbour El Salvador was already strong before the football competition that provided the final trigger for military conflict. The immediate setting was indeed a set of qualifying matches for the 1970 World Cup.

The two Central American countries met for the first game in the Honduran capital of Tegucigalpa on June 8, 1969, which Honduras won 1–0. Fighting between rival fans took place. The second match, on June 15, 1969 in the Salvadoran capital of San Salvador, was won 3–0 by El Salvador. This was followed by even greater rioting.

This made a decider match necessary which took place on neutral ground in Mexico City on June 26, 1969. El Salvador won the third game 3–2 after extra time.

Later that day, a furious Salvadoran government angrily broke off all diplomatic ties with Honduras, but the mood

created by the football against a hated neighbour was just the trigger, and the Salvadoran statement for its reasons for taking such drastic action made this clear.

The dispute was about migration, poverty and land. For much of the 20th century, hungry Salvadorans had been migrating to much less overpopulated Honduras and settling as peasant farmers. Now they were being evicted as refugees to an already over-crowded El Salvador, so the Honduran government could give their unofficially occupied land to people born in Honduras. The Salvadoran government and people were furious at the way this was being carried out. Some youngsters had been born in Honduras, and there were many marriages between the nationalities.

So when the diplomatic ties were broken off, El Salvador said: 'The government of Honduras has not taken any effective measures to punish these crimes which constitute genocide, nor has it given assurances of indemnification or reparations for the damages caused to Salvadorans'.

So the war wasn't entirely caused by soccer, as legend has it, nor did it erupt immediately after the game, as it claimed. It wasn't until July 14 that serious military conflict started.

San Salvador was put on full black-out while bomber aircraft – well in fact passenger planes with explosives tied to the side which could be released – attacked Toncontin International Airport, which left the Honduran Air Force (pictured above with troops on parade) unable to respond. The Salvadoran army invaded Honduras along two route, and artillery and armour was involved. It looked like they threatened the capital, Tegucigalpa.

Meanwhile the Honduran air force finally hit back on July 16, bombing an air base and oil depots. It was, by the way, the last war in which piston-engined (ie not jet) fighters fought each other, including some World War II vintage aircraft. Corsairs and Mustangs took part.

Intense diplomatic pressure from the Organisation of American States brought a cease-fire on July 18. The refugee problem got only worse, and the poverty this caused contributed directly to the El Salvador Civil War, about ten years later.

The immediate cost on the Soccer War was about 300,000 refugees, some 900 killed on the El Salvador side, and about 2,250 on the Honduran side, including 250 troops. The Soccer War solved nothing, achieved nothing, and made the suffering and poverty at the root of the conflict worse.

THE 30-YEAR RHODODENDRON WAR: In February 2017, an Irish politician gave an impassioned speech about out-of-control shrubbery. 'The rhododendron situation in Killarney National Park has gotten so bad, minister,' Michael Healy-Rae declared from the floor of the Irish parliament, 'nothing short of calling in the army is going to put it right.'

It turned out that the Irish state had been waging war – using horses, tractors, chains, poison spray, flame-throwers – for 30 years on *Rhododendron ponticum*, a plant that was relatively restrained in the Himalayan uplands but just went bonkers when introduced to the humid climate and acidic soils of western Britain and Ireland, where the dense shrub has few natural predators or serious competitors. Its leaves are, after all, poisonous to animals, so why would they eat it?

Its foliage is so thick that nothing grows underneath. In 2014, two experienced hillwalkers had to be rescued when they became trapped in a thicket of it. Well, frankly, one has a feeling of doom about this whole thing – like the Great Emu War at the start of this chapter.

2 LONG AND SHORT WARS

THE 38-MINUTE WAR: Was between Great Britain and Zanzibar on August 27, 1896, and as well as being remarkably quick, epitomized gunboat diplomacy – literally – and British Imperial power at its zenith. Thus as well as high-handed regime change, it brought an end to slavery in that island Sultanate off East Africa. It also illustrated the massive resources the Royal Navy – the biggest the world had ever seen – could call on all round the globe.

The immediate cause was the death of the pro-British Sultan, Hamad bin Thuwaini on August 25 and the succession of Sultan

Khalid bin Barghash who was more hostile to Britain and possibly pro-German. The trouble was that a Treaty signed between the two countries a few years before required the British Consul to approve the new Sultan. The Consul issued an ultimatum to Khalid to leave the palace by 9am on the 27th. He didn't.

Meanwhile the Consul gathered a formidable fleet – three cruisers, two gunboats, 1,590 Marines, and 900 pro-British Zanzibarian troops. Defending the Palace were about 2,800 troops, two artillery pieces and some machine guns. Oddly enough the Zanzibarian Navy – an armed royal yacht called *HHS Glasgow* (pictured) – was anchored amidst the British fleet. Firing started as promised after the 9am ultimatum expired, and the Palace was soon on fire, the Sultan's flag shot down and the royal yacht, which was firing a few cannon, sunk. The Sultan's harem (pictured right) took a

THE HAREM AFTER THE BOMBARDMENT.

particular hammering. It was all over by 9.40 as the surviving defenders fled, the Sultan to the German consulate. Casualties on the defending side were heavy – 500 killed or wounded – but only one British sailor was wounded. The shortest war in history was over in 38 minutes.

The sailors of the *Glasgow* clambered up the masts as she sat on the bottom of the harbour, and were quickly rescued by the British. For many years afterwards the masts poking out of the water were a familiar navigation feature to look out for (below).

The British even made Sultan Khalid's supporters pay for the ammunition they had expended.

The Sultan escaped from the German consulate by bringing a German warship alongside and using a plank between the two so he never had to leave German territory, and a new Sultan – a semi-colonial puppet government – was installed. But things improved, slavery was abolished, and peace reigned for 67 years. Eventually after independence, Tanganyika and Zanzibar merged to form the modern independent country of Tanzania in 1964.

SUPPLEMENT TO THE GRAPHIC, October 11, 1896.

FORTY MINUTES' WORK AT ZANZIBAR

FINAL PHOTOGRAPHS OF THE TOWN TAKEN AFTER THE BOMBARDMENT

THE MASTS AND FUNNEL OF THE ZANZIBARI EXECUTIVE "GLASGOW," WHICH WAS SUNK IN THE HARBOUR DURING THE ENGAGEMENT

Press reports from the time. The top picture shows the sunken Zanzibarian royal yacht *HHS Glasgow*. Two other small launches were also sunk in the unequal battle

FRIDAY, AUGUST 28, 1896.

AT ZANZIBAR.

It took rather less than an hour, yesterday, for Her MAJESTY'S warships to reduce the Palace at Zanzibar to ashes and the false SULTAN to subjection. The affair was very briskly carried

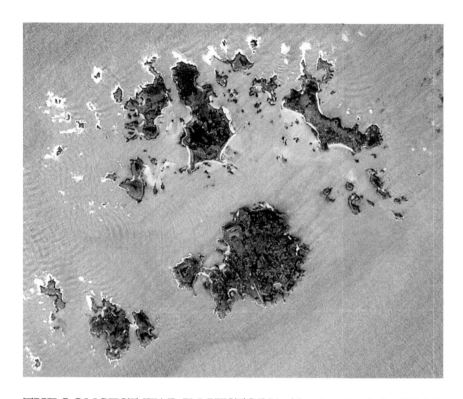

THE LONGEST WAR IN HISTORY: Also involved the British. But, unlike the shortest war, above, it caused fewer casualties. In fact, none.

For 335 years this war was fought – or rather, not fought as everyone had forgotten about it – between the Isles of Scilly (south-west of Cornwall, aerial photograph above) and the Netherlands.

It was an official war, however. It happened because of the English Civil War (1642-52), of the parliamentary Roundheads versus the royalist Cavaliers. The Royalists were losing, so were eventually driven out of the mainland Cornwall to the Scilly Isles, taking a small navy with them.

The Dutch, who had escaped Spanish domination with English help over the previous century, sided with the English parliamentarians. This meant they were the enemy to the Scilly garrison, who used their small navy to raid passing Dutch ships and get much-needed supplies.

In March 1651, the Dutch Admiral Maarten Tromp arrived in the Scillies to demand reparation for these shipping raids and an end to

them. He was sent away without a satisfactory answer.

Tromp was recorded in April 1651, on landing in Cornwall, as having declared war on the Scillies. This was not a light-hearted matter – the Dutch had a formidable and aggressive navy (above) which had fought the English recently and would so do again soon. No mere bombardment with Edam cheeses!

However in June that year the English Navy, under parliamentary control, arrived under Admiral Robert Blake and took possession of the islands. The Dutch sailed home, problem solved.

No one ever bothered to make a peace treaty as the Scillies were no longer a separate country.

Move on to 1985, and the chairman of the Scilly Isles Council, Roy Duncan (pictured), was fed up with hearing the 'myth' that they were still at war with the Dutch. He wrote to the Netherlands Embassy in London to debunk the idea.

They found they *were* still at war, technically. The Dutch ambassador Jonkheer Rein Heydecoper was asked to visit and sign a peace treaty, which he gamely did on April 17, 1986. He joked that it must have been rather harrowing for the Scillonians all those years 'to know that we could have attacked at any moment.' At last the islanders could sleep soundly. What a Scilly state of affairs!

3 DISASTROUSLY STUPID WARS

THE POINTLESS PARAGUAYAN WAR: This war of 1864 was one of the most staggeringly stupid and horribly costly of all those in this book. In fact the worst war in South American history – with an estimated 400,000 deaths – was completely pointless.

The war of 1864-70 started with Paraguay's needless aggression against its bigger neighbours, Brazil, Uruguay and Argentina, who formed a triple alliance against it. The cited cause was some imagined border dispute, but it was the delusional, vainglorious leadership of President Solano Lopez that was the real cause.

Even when roundly defeated in the field, the Paraguayans carried on a costly guerrilla war for years. In scenes to be recreated in the Soviet Union in World War II, soldiers were asked to charge into battle unarmed, with the chance of picking up weapons from the fallen. They were also urged to kill any comrades, even officers, who talked of surrender. Cavalry had to eat their own horses to stay alive. And retreat involved destroying the locals, crops, foodstuffs and anything of value.

When their lunatic President Solano Lopez (pictured) was finally cornered and killed on March 1, 1870, he died shouting: '¡Muero con mi patria!' ('I die with my homeland!'), which was nearly true, as probably most of his countrymen had perished in the war. Estimates vary but suggest up to 69 per cent of the population was lost, and up to 90 per cent of the young males. These are the higher end estimates, but even so the slaughter seemed even more appalling than the then recent U.S. Civil War which was terrible enough.

Photos exist of piles of bodies at some of the 21 battles – we won't share them here – but diseases such as cholera and sepsis seemed to have made huge impacts on the various armies involved.

For example a whole battalion of thirsty Brazilian troops died after drinking from an infected river.

However vague the figures for Paraguayan losses, the triple alliance certainly lost 140,000. The survivors in Paraguay were thrown into abject poverty for decades. All for nothing.

THE PASTRY WAR: Yes, really! Known in Spanish as the *Guerra de los pasteles*, or in French – and it involved them too – as *Guerre des Pâtisseries*. In fact no fewer than six nations had a slice of this pointless 1830s war, which started over a complaint about just one bakery, and never seemed to be about much else.

Neverthless, it cost 127 lives and left 189 wounded, so it was far from half-baked. It soured relations between France and Mexico for decades – the war flared up again for a second helping in 1861, and normal relations did not resume until 1880.

The original complaint was over a small bakery shop run by a Frenchman at Tacubaya, near Mexico City. Many other properties had been damaged in civil unrest at about this time but the owner of

101

the shop, a Frenchman named Remontel, decided to complain to the King of France, Louis Philippe.

Far away in Paris, if he had had a *soupçon* of common sense, the king would have declined to get involved in such a petty complaint so far, far away.

French forces in the Pastry War bombard a Mexican fort at Veracruz (Vernet)

But then pastries, and bread, are pretty important to the French, – even if the late Marie Antoinette hadn't really said: 'let them eat cake' a few years before. Now the French monarchy had been restored, it seemed – absurdly – a matter of national honour.

Reparations for the supposed damage to the shop were demanded. In fact quite a lot of dough, as it were, was sought – 600,000 pesos, at a time when a Mexican workman's daily wage was one peso. After the French king failed to get any answer from the Mexicans, he decided to send a war fleet.

One wants a Pastry War ordered by the French upper crust to be one involving *croissant* catapults and charging with fixed *baguettes*, the odd chocolate *bombe* rolling across a deck – but this was to be a real shooting war.

A French fleet arrived in November 1838 and blockaded the Mexican coast, and bombarded a fortress off Veracruz. By December the French had captured the whole city, so the Mexicans had reluctantly to declare war.

Now it gets more complicated – the United States, which logic suggests would be on the side of residents of America against a colonial European power – side with France *against* the Mexicans.

The British, oddly, join the Mexican cause. And Texas, still an independent republic, wades in against Mexico. None of these powers actually do any fighting at this point, but the U.S. sends a warship to help the French blockade the Mexican coast.

The Mexicans try to get round the blockade by smuggling in supplies from the Republic of Texas. Authorities there clamp down on the contraband, and in one raid discover 100 barrels of white powder left on the shoreline by fleeing smugglers. It is flour, aptly, for bakeries. That bit of the Texan city of Corpus Christi is known as Flour Bluff today as a result.

Enter a larger-than-life character by the name of (take a deep breath) Antonio de Padua María Severino López de Santa Anna y Pérez de Lebrón (pictured). Called Tony by his friends, one almost wants to add after such a florid title, but in fact he was known as Santa Anna and was a huge character in this era of Mexico's war of independence against Spain, and later the war to keep its rebelling provinces, one of which had become Texas (where as you know, nothing secedes like success).

Santa Anna had been President of Mexico a few times – three times, briefly, in 1833, for example, each time swapping with the same politician – but was known better as a strong military leader against the new nation's enemies. He was called 'Saviour of the Nation' and 'Napoleon of the West' – mainly by himself, it must be said, but the titles caught on. He had fought both *against* and *for* Mexican independence, and had been a conservative, a liberal, a republican and a royalist at different stages, so he was consistent only in one thing – about being a self-proclaimed national hero.

At this point he was in retirement and in semi-disgrace for having lost Texas but was still the most famous fighter/politician the country had ever had. If he joined in, even a Pastry War, it's a recipe for drama, and Santa Anna is soon leading the army from the front. He has his leg wounded by French grapeshot, and has to have it amputated in the field.

Like Britain's Lord Uxbridge a few years earlier at Waterloo, Santa Anna has his leg buried with full military honours. And also like Uxbridge – who became Marquis of Anglesey – he has several false legs made and fights on, militarily and politically, for many years.

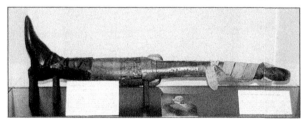

One of his legs (pictured) even gets captured by the Americans and used, somewhat disrespectfully, as a baseball bat. The 4th Illinois Infantry never did return it and it can be seen in their museum today. His replacement leg is also on show in Mexico, so just like the Marquis of Anglesey, there are three monuments to the same leg. Like Uxbridge, Santa Anna had the dubious option of attending part of his own funeral. (Recall the wonderful exchange at Waterloo while Wellington was on his horse observing the French with a telescope. Uxbridge, who had been standing alongside: 'By Gord, Sir, I've lorst a leg.' Wellington glances down and says: 'So you have, Uxbridge' and calmly resumes looking through his telescope). Both men became known – sorry about this – as leg ends in their own life time!

You might have thought Santa Anna would be hopping mad about losing his leg to the French, but in fact they did him a massive favour and it gave him a leg to stand on, as it were, to regain power. He never lost an opportunity to remind the Mexican people that he'd already laid down at least part of his body in their defence. In the chaotic, revolving-door politics, he was president ten times.

At this point the British intervene, diplomatically, to restore some kind of sanity. The French withdraw after being promised 600,000 pesos by the Mexicans, although this can have been only a fraction of the cost of the whole absurd expedition, which collapsed like a half-baked soufflé.

The Mexicans never pay it so the French (by now led by another vainglorious royal, Emperor Napoleon III) go for a second helping of Pastry War, launching another attack on Mexico in 1861, waging a huge campaign involving an invading army, installing their own man as Emperor Maximilian I. The French are eventually beaten back, and after a rising, their man Maximilian (above) is soon toast – he was shot by firing squad in 1867.

Which all goes to show that you cannot shrug off the importance of French *pâtisserie*. The Pastry War was no mere *hors d'oeuvre* of history, but ended up being the *entrée* to a wider conflict. And that vainglorious leaders, sometimes, get their just deserts.

The execution of Emperor Maximilian, as depicted by Manet

The above two chapters were free extract from a book by the same author, entitled MADCAP MILITARY MAYHEM. While we thought readers might enjoy that at no additional cost, none of this at times light-hearted history should detract from the deeply serious subject of Part One of this book.

PEARL HARBOR
DECEMBER 7, 1941, A DATE
WHICH WILL LIVE IN INFAMY...
NO MATTER HOW LONG IT
MAY TAKE US TO OVERCOME
THIS PREMEDITATED INVASION,
THE AMERICAN PEOPLE, IN
THEIR RIGHTEOUS MIGHT,
WILL WIN THROUGH
TO ABSOLUTE VICTORY.
PRESIDENT FRANKLIN D. ROOSEVELT

ABOUT THE AUTHOR

Benedict le Vay is a London-born journalist, author and 'rather bad yachtsman and potter' who has worked as a sub-editor in major newspapers in Britain, Hong Kong and New Zealand. A father of two, his books have included the best-selling *Eccentric Britain, Eccentric London, Eccentric Oxford* and *Eccentric Cambridge* guides, and also *Britain From The Rails: A Window-Gazer's Guide*, all published by Bradt, plus *Weeping Waters: When Train Meets Volcano* about a New Zealand disaster and *The Secret History of Everyday Stuff: Astounding, Fascinating or Remarkable Facts About Your Everyday Life,* both available from Amazon. Asked if he himself is eccentric, he says: 'Not at all, I'm afraid. The best I can do is being Honorary Secretary of the Friends of the A272, and asking for my ashes to be blasted from the chimney of my favourite steam loco at my funeral. But then hasn't everyone?'

Picture: WENDY FULLER

BEST-SELLERS BY THE SAME AUTHOR

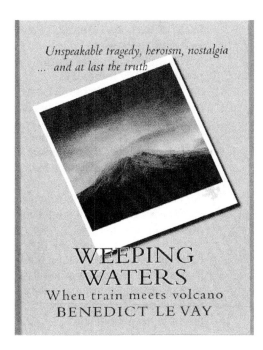

Unspeakable tragedy, heroism, nostalgia ... and at last the truth

WEEPING WATERS
When train meets volcano
BENEDICT LE VAY

Published on Amazon. Press reviews:

Sixty years on, le Vay's masterly reconstruction is a fine memorial.- *Jane Mays, Daily Mail, London*

He has researched the story well and tells it with great passion, making the full facts public for the first time. - *The Railway Magazine, UK.*

International must-read. - *Dominion-Post, Wellington, New Zealand*

THE SECRET HISTORY OF EVERYDAY STUFF
ASTOUNDING, FASCINATING OR REMARKABLE FACTS ABOUT YOUR DAILY LIFE

BENEDICT LE VAY

Published on Amazon. Real reader reviews:

If you have an enquiring mind for all things trivia then this book is for you. Full to the brim of unusual and witty facts about anything and everything. Well worth the money.

Mr Le Vay has a nose for the odd and the curious, and in this excellent book digs up facts that answer the questions we have all, in our idler moments, asked ourselves.

A great read. Some really eye opening facts and written with a good sense of humour. Great for adults and kids.

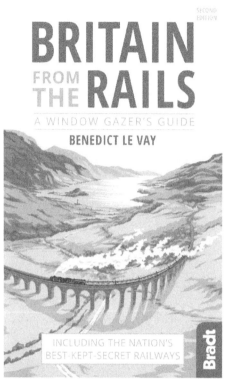

Published by Bradt. Real reader reviews:

Bought this as a Christmas present for my father. He describes it as "one of the best books I have ever read". This is an incredible statement as my father is an academic who has read more books than anyone else I know - and written a few historical/church books himself. He hasn't let the book out of his sight since receiving it yesterday afternoon.

Now, finally, the network has a book to be proud of - I love how Benedict le Vay gives a detailed explanation on a huge variety of railway lines throughout the country, be it main line, commuter or country branch lines, but always with a good smattering of humour in there to make you want to read on

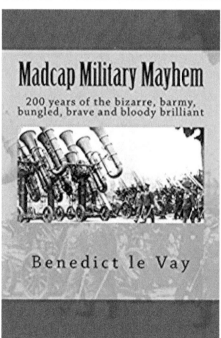

Published on Amazon. Real reader reviews:

Wry, informative, quirky, this book is a pleasing lucky-dip of information about military mishaps and ideas. I did not know Stukas were so flawed. One learns about odd inventions such as the deadly adaptation of a Vespa scooter and the pre-radar attempts to use sound for early warning systems. Broken down into small entries, it is a perfect bedtime or loo book. Good fun.

Bought this as a gift but can't stop reading interesting facts. I thoroughly recommend it for anyone interested in Military History and Trivia.

LATEST BOOK FROM THE SAME AUTHOR

Printed in Great Britain
by Amazon

18996341R00068